Who Will Wind the Clock?

Margaret Jensen
author of *First We Have Coffee*

HARVEST HOUSE PUBLISHERS
Eugene, Oregon 97402

78

Except where otherwise indicated, all Scripture quotations in this book are taken from the King James Version of the Bible.

Cover by Left Coast Design, Portland, Oregon

WHO WILL WIND THE CLOCK?

Copyright ©1993 by Margaret Tweten Jensen
Published by Harvest House Publishers
Eugene, Oregon 97402

Library of Congress Cataloging-in-Publication Data

Jensen, Margaret T. (Margaret Tweten), 1916–
  Who will wind the clock? / Margaret Jensen.
    p. c.m.
  Originally published: Nashville : T. Nelson, ©1993.
  ISBN 0-7369-0003-9
  1. Jensen, Harold Edward, 1912-1991. 2. Clergy—United States—Biography.
  3. Jensen, Margaret T. (Margaret Tweten), 1916- . 4. Christian biography—
  United States. I. Title.
  [BR1725.J429J43 1999]
  248.8'66'092—dc21   98-37466
  [B]   CIP

Printed in the United States of America.

99 00 01 02 03 04 / BC / 10 9 8 7 6 5 4 3 2 1

Dedicated to our daughter, Janice Dawn Jensen Carlberg, better known as Jan.

Jan, a daughter of joy, brought honor to her parents, loving fun to her brothers Dan and Ralph, and helped create a special relationship with her new sister Chris, Ralph's wife.

Today, as the wife of Dr. Judson Carlberg, President of Gordon College, Jan brings the same love, joy, and faithfulness that has marked her journey with God from early childhood.

Her book, *The Hungry Heart*, reflects her love for God's Word.

Not only is she the loving mother of Heather and Chad, but her heart also embraces the students of Gordon College, and all her extended family. "Aunt Jan" is special to her nieces and nephews as well as to those adopted along the way.

Through our wilderness journey she was always "Daddy's girl," who believed in the Promised Land.

In her extensive traveling, speaking and writing, she reflects a compassion and understanding that comes from learning in the valley.

Dedicated also to Ralph Harold Jensen, our youngest son, who came through his own wilderness wanderings to the love of the heavenly Father and back into the arms of his earthly father. God turned Ralph's heart home, then gave him Chris, a gift of love to our entire family.

Remembering his lonely teenage years, Ralph's gift to his children, Shawn, Eric, Sarah and Kathryn, is, "I'm always here for you." He is there for all the games—and he is there to listen to the cries in the night.

Through a special gift from God, "The Master's Touch," Ralph is able to take rough wood strengthened by the storms of life and fashion beautiful eighteenth-century furniture reproductions.

"Just so God takes us, wounded in the storms, and makes something beautiful out of our lives."

Harold and Ralph were inseparable during the fourteen years in Wilmington—then Harold went Home.

Jan and Ralph, and their families, surround me with the love that never lets go. It is with deep thanks to God that this book of sorrow and joy is dedicated to Janice and Ralph.

Contents

A Time for Thanks

- A special thanks to my grandchildren, Heather and Chad Carlberg and Shawn, Eric, Sarah, and Kathryn Jensen, for their cheering on the sidelines, and for their saying—and living—"Grammy, we will always be there for you."

- To Jud Carlberg, Jan's husband, who always has a "thumbs up—go for it" kind of encouragement.

- To Chris, Ralph's wife, who packs books, travels endless miles, makes sure I have my plane ticket—and matching shoes.

- A special thanks to Les Stobbe and the Here's Life family for believing in an unknown "Grammy"—faith in action. And to the Harvest House family, who picked up where Here's Life left off.

- To Wayne Hastings, and to Jim Warren of Prime Time America, both urging "one more book."

- I thank God for my church family, Myrtle Grove Presbyterian Church, Wilmington, North Carolina, and our faithful pastors, Horace Hilton, pastor emeritus, Rev. Stephen Crotts, Senior Minister, and Jim Glasgow, for their love and prayers that follow me across the miles.

- To Linda Britton who transferred my yellow pads to the computer, probably praying (like Harold did) for the gift of interpretation.

- To the "Royal Guard," my sisters Grace, Doris, Joyce and Jeanelle, who march boldly in step to the throne of grace to ask for help in the time of need. Now Grace and Jeanelle are a part of the "cloud of witnesses" joining Harold in the cheering section.

- Thank you, all my wonderful friends at home and abroad, for the letters and calls bringing encouragement, love, and prayers across the miles. What a family we have!

- Thank you, Dan, for being the loving, obedient son whose steadfastness never wavered during the changing years of long ago. We hold those memories deep in our hearts. We love you, Danny Boy.

"Death is not extinguishing the light. It is putting out the lamp because dawn has come."

—Source Unknown

"Some things are ruined when broken, but the heart is at its best when broken."

—Source Unknown

Give me, O Lord, a steadfast heart,
    which no unworthy affection may drag downward;
Give me an unconquered heart,
    which no tribulation can wear out;
Give me an upright heart,
    which no unworthy purpose my tempt aside.
Bestow on me also, O Lord my God,
    understanding to know you, diligence to seek you,
        wisdom to find you,
    and a faithfulness that may finally embrace you
    through Jesus Christ our Lord.

—Thomas Aquinas

Foreword

I have this thought: A significant lot of the younger generations have never grasped the fact that life is much more like a roller coaster ride (a certainty of ups and downs) and much less like a straight-line success story that goes from good to better to best.

My dear friend, Margaret Jensen, makes this point well. The aforementioned "significant lot" need to sit at her feet and listen. The stories she tells—and this book includes many of them—are marked with dreams and despair, joys and pain, living and dying, love and hate. In other words, raw life: sometimes coarse and demanding; sometimes colorful and fun . . . and lots of something in between. And after this significant lot heard what Margaret had to say, they would conclude that it's only in the final years of this phase of eternal life that we find out if people have truly lived well and if we really understand what prosperity is.

I know Margaret Jensen well. She exudes a beauty not only of spirit but also of face. While Margaret is somewhat "north of forty" in terms of age and in that stage of life when a shallow society ceases to talk of physical attractiveness, she is nevertheless beautiful to look at. Chalk it up to lovely Scandinavian features and smart grooming if you wish. But I think the stories have made the difference.

This book will tell you why I think this. The appealing woman who often stands before crowds of people and makes them alternately laugh and weep as she tells her stories and suggests what the stories mean is neither the product of some public relations firm nor a drama coach. No, she is rather a picture of what God can do when someone chooses to spend his/her years facing life standing up, bearing the pain and harvesting the blessings without being distracted by either.

When I was a child, we used to sing a song whose melody was perhaps poorly written music and whose words, for the most part, were poor poetry. Nevertheless, even though I haven't sung the song for decades, a couplet in the chorus has stuck with me. "When the road is rough and steep, fix your eyes upon Jesus.. .." That my friend Margaret does, and that is the secret of her internal and external beauty.

Read this book and you will see how a champion faces life. You will note that in the times of stress there is no whining, complaining, or claiming "victim" that we have grown used to hearing today. Sure, there is the confession of profound sadness and loneliness, and the desire, on occasion, to strike back. After all, Margaret is very inch a human being, and so was Harold (her deceased husband), and so are the Jensen kids. But during the downturns of the roller coaster, there is something else: the overarching theme of perseverance, stamina and brute faithfulness. Of these we need to hear more.

In the upturns of the Jensen stories? Thankfulness and humility, and the seizing of opportunities. The ability to "seize the day," as they now say, wringing out of it every drop of God's favor.

Read the chapters of this book carefully. Note the moments when a man and woman faced hatred on the streets, stress in their marriage, anguish and delight in their children, self-doubt within. And then tell me that is not the real life that we are all facing in our own roller coaster rides.

What excites me as I read these stories is my personal knowledge of the author. I am old enough to have traced the careers of beautiful movie stars, successful politicians, champion athletes—our symbols of modern prosperity. Can I be frank? Too many of them are handling the endgame of their lives in graceless, bitter, lonely, unattractive ways.

I see the way Margaret Jensen is handling the endgame of her life: busy, enthusiastic, generous, grace-giving, and optimistic. Where has she found the ways and means to do this? The answer, I think, is in the stories. How she lived through the ones you're about to read defines how she is living now. Listen carefully: You're about to uncover some wonderful beauty tips.

—Gordon MacDonald
Lexington, Massachusetts

Margaret and Harold, July 1991

1

The Winter of the Soul

The long line of cars followed slowly behind the white hearse. Jan and I rode in silence, the first car in line. It was grey.

Around us tall pines stood like sentinels in the surrounding woods, and the sun pierced the white clouds floating across the blue skies of Wilmington, North Carolina.

"I'm glad the hearse carrying my Daddy is white; I never did like black. Remember going to Orlando to the Bookseller's Convention and how I followed Daddy's car?"

I remembered. Jan and thirteen-year-old Sarah had sat in the front seat of my blue Pontiac while Chris, Sarah's mother, curled up in the back seat to get some needed sleep. Harold, my husband of fifty-three years, sat in the front seat of his grey Oldsmobile, and Kathryn, ten, watched from the rear to be sure our blue car continued following. Such a short time ago.

Now our daughter Jan and I were in the grey car, and Ralph, our son, was following with his family—his wife Chris, and their children Sarah, Kathryn, Eric and Shawn.

Jan's husband, Jud Carlberg, came next with their children, Heather and Chad, and their friends, Kris and Jeremy.

Harold was "Papa" to his adoring grandchildren as well as to all the others he had adopted along the way.

The magnificent live oaks bent their branches over the meandering road.

> Tall trees in sorrow bend . . .
> You can't go home again.[1]

This quote filtered through the back roads of my mind.

Jan broke the silence. "I never dreamed I would ever follow Daddy like this."

The cars eased along the road while the dogwoods cried their tears into the wind, and the pines mourned as the wind turned cold on that beautiful autumn day, November 4, 1991.

Harold again was in the lead, this time to be buried in the Oleander Gardens of Wilmington, and I wondered for a moment how long a person could live with grief that tears the heart apart.

I knew the beauty of fall would never be the same. Grief like a cold wind would blow the leaves from the oak trees, and my tears would fall like the red leaves of the dogwoods.

The winter of the soul had come, too soon, and without warning.

2

The Grey Dawn

I wondered how many times I would relive the morning Harold died in my arms.

Night after night I would hear his call, "Margaret, help me!"

Like a shot I was out of bed, running into the bathroom where Harold was leaning over the sink.

"My back!"

I knew he had pulled a lawn mower out of the shed the day before so I thought it was a strained muscle.

"No, this is different. I can't breathe."

"Let me get you on the bed."

Oh, Jesus, touch him! Relieve this pain. Oh, Jesus, touch him!

I eased him onto the bed, praying while I held him. Then he was quiet.

"Oh, Harold, has the pain gone?"

He didn't answer.

He was gone!

He looked so peaceful.

Then I cried, "Jesus, help me!"

It was 5 a.m., October 31, 1991.

Chris answered the phone. "Tell Ralph to come," I sobbed, and hung up.

Ralph held me in his arms as they took Harold away. Inside, my entire being screamed, "Don't leave me; I can't make it alone. I don't even know how to wind the grandfather clock."

Ralph sobbed, "Daddy, Daddy." We clung together like frightened children, alone in the grey dawn.

Then abruptly, Ralph said, "Mama, let us thank God for what we know, not what we see. We know God is sovereign and Daddy is Home with Him. He died so peacefully, right in your arms. We know God's purposes are right."

"I know. I know. And I'll always be so thankful that I was right here."

I put the coffeepot on; then we began reading Psalm 27. "The LORD is my light and my salvation . . ." and I won't be afraid.

But I was afraid!

"Don't talk to Jan, Ralph. Talk to Jud first."

Oh, how I wanted to spare her the news, but grief comes to us all and we can only comfort each other as God gives comfort.

Comfort did come! When Chris came, she plunged into the practical: beds to make, bathrooms to clean, endless telephone calls.

The first ones at our door were the Hiltons, God's faithful servants. They were always there when anyone needed them. They came with their love and prayers, and their tears, and God's peace enveloped us like a security blanket.

"Like a mighty army moves the Church of God."

This amazing universal family that the world will never understand, the Church, the people of God, came with their hearts and hands, and with compassionate arms they enfolded us in a love that is beyond human understanding.

I am glad I'm a member of the family of God. That day we needed our extended family.

The pink hue of morning slipped into the dawn and dispersed its greyness. Throughout that tear-filled day the grandfather clock sounded its clear message that some things never change.

I would learn how to wind the clock, and each Saturday morning I would do it, just like Harold did.

With the familiar sound of the clock I was reminded once again that our times are in God's hands, and He winds life's clock.

I would trust His hand to wind my clock.

3

The Protective Wall

"Paulie pushed the button! Paulie pushed the button! The casket's going down!"

"He didn't mean to. It was an accident. Aunt Jan was explaining about the big hole and how the casket would be lowered."

The wide-eyed cousins stood frozen in their tracks until an attendant stopped the casket's premature descent into the gaping hole.

"We were all looking in the hole wondering how papa would rise from the grave when Paulie accidentally pushed the button." Kathryn (Katie) usually had an explanation for everything. "The Bible says the dead in Christ shall rise first and we wondered how Papa would get out of that hole."

The young cousins gazed into the hole and discussed the obvious theology: "God will have to figure that out."

They were all there—the aunts, the uncles, the older and the younger cousins.

An SOS always brought the five Tweten sisters together. When news of joy hit the telephone wires we all rejoiced together. The last time we had a fun reunion Harold printed a sign and hung it on the clothesline: "The Sisters Are Coming—HELP!"

When sorrow invaded the happy households, we wept together.

So they came! Jeanelle, the youngest, from Washington, D.C., Joyce the songbird from Arkansas, Doris from Stoneville, and Grace from Greensboro. They were there like oaks of righteousness.

Harold's brothers Howard and Jack were there, along with a new brother who had joined them, Peter Stam.

The church family, all our adopted children, our friends and neighbors, all came like a protective wall.

"I found Papa's Aqua-Velva in his car, Aunt Margaret. Don't you want it?"

"It's okay, Benjamin, just put it back in the car."

"But Aunt Margaret, Papa always smelled like Aqua-Velva."

"I know!" (I bought expensive Copenhagen cologne for my big Dane, and he still used Aqua-Velva.)

Benjamin trotted back to the car to put the cologne back in Papa's container, along with the mouthwash and a comb. (He always had that meticulously dressed look, even when going to the grocery store.)

One of Ralph's employees was sobbing—hard, choking sobs.

I put my arms around him. "It's okay to cry, but remember how he always said how smart you were, and that you could do anything."

He remembered! All his life he had been told how worthless he was, then Harold came and convinced him he could do anything he wanted to. And he did! He kept crying. "Oh, I hurt; I really hurt. I loved that man."

"My dad built dreams for others," Ralph said at the memorial service, "even if his own dreams were unfulfilled. He always came along to build dreams for others."

Slowly the crowd retreated to their cars and then it was our turn. Leaving the lonely grave with the yellow lilies reminded us that spring and resurrection follow the winter of the soul.

I could hear our beloved Pastor Emeritus, Horace Hilton: "When we look at the ocean it seems to end at the sky, but if we took a boat and kept going, we'd touch another shore—that's a picture of death."

Our young pastor, Jim Glasgow, read: "Let not your heart be troubled: ye believe in God, believe also in me" (John 14:1). Life-giving words!

"I feel like I've been to a great concert," a friend commented. "Homer McKeithen's powerful baritone voice sang the great hymns of faith into the hearts of the people."

It was a time to weep over their own broken dreams and draw comfort into the wounded places.

When the cars pulled into our driveway, the women of the church were there to serve the crowd with beautifully set up buffets.

"Grammy, your neighbor, Miss Clara, pulled up in her golf cart with a crock of homemade soup." Leave it to Miss Clara, the original.

Later, the cousins, the grandchildren, and all their friends found places on the floor to join the other relatives and friends. Homer led the singing, the language of the soul: the great hymns of faith, a reminder that God is changeless. Then the choruses followed—hand-clapping, foot-stomping, camp-meeting songs.

We laughed and cried but the songs filled the empty places and brought joy that brings strength—then hope.

It was midnight when the cars turned homeward and all became quiet. The lonely grey car stood beside the blue one. I remembered a long time ago when nine-year-old Ralph had burst into the kitchen. "I know what it means to die, Mama. The driver goes to heaven—that's the soul. And the car, the body, can't go any more."

The body was buried in a lonely grave, but the driver was Home—safe!

"Mom," Jan remembered later, "do you realize we sat, laughed, and shared wonderful memories until midnight? If someone passed by our house that person would probably have said, 'I wonder what wonderful thing happened in that home.'"

The wonderful thing?

"Amazing grace! How sweet the sound."

4

The Paint Shoes

"Where is my sister?" Joyce hunted through the house, and Jan suggested I might be in the garage.

I was. Holding a pair of old paint shoes, I stood in the garage crying my heart out.

Joyce cried with me; then Jan came and we all cried over Harold's old paint shoes.

"He worked so hard to paint everything just right." Harold's painting left no room for splash. My talent had more splash than smooth. When I needed cabinets painted I'd use my old trick: "Think I'll get some paint and start on the inside."

"Oh, no, Margaret, promise me you won't paint. It takes more work to clean up after you. Just tell me what you want and I'll get to it."

And I'd promise! Of course, I had no intention of painting anything. My trick always worked.

So it came to pass that Harold painted—and painted—and since he was the perfectionist, it was done right.

Now I stood holding his paint shoes and crying. Joyce, with her sensitive wisdom, said, "Put the paint shoes on the shelf and let's go out and dig a memorial garden."

We put the paint shoes on the shelf and took a shovel, hoe, and rake, and began a memorial garden.

My friend Anna brought a bag of bulbs. "Plant these, and think of Harold, spring, and resurrection."

We did. "Look at all the mums friends have sent. Let's sort the colors and plant them like a work of art."

They did other little things, too, to help. Doris saw my old dish drainer looking a little "gross," so she bought a new one.

When sadness slipped through the door, Jeanelle sat down at the piano and Grace sang, "It matters to Him about you." Joyce is really the soloist, but Grace knew this was the time to sing.

So she sang.

We hung together like clothes on a line. No one wanted to leave.

Eventually, though, everyone had to return home. The college grandchildren had been excused from exams and now had to return to their classes. They had seen their fun-loving family rejoice at our fiftieth wedding anniversary celebration. Then, three years later, their beloved Papa was gone. But they saw the family as one, and they heard the songs in the night.

Chad, the eldest grandson, said it well. "We loved our Papa and laughed at his jokes, his Aqua-Velva, and powder on the toilet seat. He was there for all of us."

Now they were going back to the classroom, but what they learned about life and death was not in a textbook. They heard us sing!

Jan and I were alone now—our wonderful daughter of joy, Daddy's special girl.

We had to go through papers, pay bills, change names, check legal documents. And then the insurance! Robert Bale spent hours going over papers. Most of the insurance expired when Harold turned sixty-nine—Harold was seventy-nine.

I was glad I had memorized Philippians 4:19. Here's my special paraphrase: My God shall supply all your needs—not according to Harold's insurance—but according to God's riches in Christ Jesus.

I felt panic, but then peace.

The bank, the lock-box, the Social Security changes —they overwhelmed me. Harold always paid the bills while I just wrote!

One day I had to get more copies of the death notice. Jan parked outside the courthouse while I ran up the steps and met a woman who recognized me as the author of *Lena*.

"Oh, I'm so glad to see you. Your book helped me through a difficult time. What are you doing here?"

I couldn't say it. I just handed her the death notice.

"Oh, no, your husband?"

I nodded.

"Oh, I am going through a most painful divorce."

Suddenly I was alert. "Oh, no. My dear, that's worse than a death."

We clung to each other on the courthouse steps and prayed. I didn't even know her name.

When I went inside, I found that the clerks also had read my books. Cheerfully they asked, "What can we do for you?"

I couldn't answer, so I handed them the death notice. "I need copies," I choked.

"Your husband?"

I nodded.

They jumped up. "Oh—we'll pray for you."

In a new way I found God's face in the most unexpected places.

When I went to the neighborhood service station I said, "I am Margaret Jensen and I have never pumped gas. I know nothing about cars."

"Ah, yes, we know who you are because your son explained how your husband took care of the car so you could write. 'Take good care of my Mama,' he said."

Within moments I was introduced to the crew and given a card with phone numbers. "Call us any time and we will help you, night or day. Don't worry about the car. You just stick to writing."

I autographed a book for each one and left with a tank of gas, oil checked, and windows washed, on my way to complete a long list of errands: printers, cleaners, photo service, office supplies, pharmacy, and grocery store.

This was the list Harold checked off, and now I wondered how I would ever have time to write again. The lists seemed endless—bank, post office, UPS, etc.

After endless hours of papers, forms, and figures, Jan had to return home—then taxes stared me in the face. Taxes? I could never even balance my checkbook. My dislike for math made me do all the figures in round numbers! I had visions of going to jail. But maybe then I could write!

The poor tax expert shook her head and wearily asked that I just leave it with her, then suggested a simple set-up for my future records.

Evening finally came, and I was alone. Shadows fell across the peaceful neighborhood and lights came on down the street. I turned the outside light on and locked the doors.

I had never been alone before! The noisy Tweten family, with three in a bed, left no time for loneliness. Then it was Harold, the children, visiting missionaries, college kids needing a place to stay—they all kept the household full of activity.

It was when the shadows of evening closed around me that I turned on all the lights.

I couldn't read; I couldn't pray; I didn't care about world news—my world had crumbled!

The hymnbook on the piano drew me to sit down and play some old hymns.

All the way my Saviour leads me;
What have I to ask beside?
Can I doubt His tender mercy,
Who through life has been my Guide?[1]

The grandfather clock struck midnight when I crawled into the king-sized bed, alone!

The teddy bear I had given to Harold last Christmas with a note, "Just hug him until I get home," sat on our bed. I reached over, pulled the bear to me and held him—and fell asleep.

The early beams of the morning streamed through the window and I recalled: "Weeping may endure for a night, but joy cometh in the morning" (Psalm 30:5).

Joy hadn't come this morning, but hope had slipped in the door.

5

The Three Pointers

The curved driveway has always been a challenge to me, and I usually back onto the lawn. Harold would turn the car around so I didn't have to wrestle with the curves—probably so I wouldn't ruin the lawn.

Now I had to back out! I had to practice, but I finally did it!

"Hurrah for Grammy! She zips out like Eric!" My cheerleaders applauded—another hurdle cleared.

"Now you need to practice getting the car into the garage." Ah, the foresight of grandchildren.

"Just go in straight. You can do it—don't hit the doors!"

The car stays in the driveway. Enough is enough!

"Eric has a game tonight so we'll pick you up and eat at K & W before the game. Okay?"

I climbed into the bleachers with the best of them and when Eric made a three-pointer I stood to my feet and cheered.

Someone tapped me on the shoulder. "Your grandson?" I nodded. How did he know?

After the game we headed to Hardee's. Eric was starved. By the time I walked into the empty house I was too tired to cry.

With thanks to God that I had made it through another day, I stopped to pray for the family, give thanks for the angels of the Lord keeping watch over the sleeping neighborhood, and especially for my friend Mildred who also knows the loneliness of an empty house.

Before I turned out the light I kissed Harold's picture good night. Sleep came quickly.

I dreamed that Harold was coming across a large room with his hand in his pocket, just like he used to do when he passed out Tootsie Rolls. He was so handsome in a light tan suit and yellow tie.

He reached for me and I ran toward him and looked up into a face of unbelievable joy.

Then I was awake. It was morning.

I called Jan. "I dreamed about Daddy and he was so happy and looked like he had been passing out Tootsie Rolls to the angels."

"Oh, Mom, that's terrific! Thank goodness he didn't have a robe and harp—he wouldn't be able to wear his ties."

We laughed together and somehow sensed that he wasn't so far away.

The dream brought a measure of peace into a new day.

Katie came bouncing in. "I dreamed about Papa. He had a raccoon puppet in his hand that was doing tricks, and he pulled my ponytail. We were all laughing. Mama called me to get up for school and I just wanted to stay with Papa. We were all around the dining room table and Papa was laughing. It was just like it used to be." Heaven seemed nearer all the time.

Chris was on the phone. "Mom, Cattie has invited all of us to spend Thanksgiving at the beach condo."

"No way! I've had Thanksgiving dinner at my house for fifty-two years, and we usually include single people with no family at hand."

A little later, Jan's loving voice came across the miles. "Mom, I heard that Cattie, your dear friend, has offered you a gift. Thanksgiving will be so different this year without Daddy, so why not make it totally different? There are times to receive. Just go!"

So it came to pass—another first.

The sun shone over the tossing sea and the ocean seemed to touch the sky. I could hear our pastor's encouragement, "If you took a boat you'd touch another shore" The peace of God enveloped Cattie's beautiful home where every window had an ocean view.

It wasn't just the delicious Thanksgiving meal; it was also the happy interaction between generations.

The young children, Faith and Catherine, Sarah and Katie, put on a program where each one had to express thanks for something. The next generation, so much a part of the stress of today's culture, knew that only in Christ could they really live meaningful lives.

Cattie and I, both alone now, could look back over the years and know, "Hitherto hath the LORD helped us" (1 Samuel 7:12). We knew what it was to weep over the lost sheep, cry in the lonely nights, and lash out against what seems so unfair, yet we still could come to grips with the sovereignty of God and the authority of God's Word. We had weathered many storms but we also remembered that the sun does shine again.

It was all there, the innocence of children at play, the struggles of youth, and the responsibilities of young parents facing the stress of holding families close while facing the world's changing economy.

There we were, Cattie and I, with our hair white, but our faith intact. We prayed that the young would see, and remember.

In one of her yesterdays, during a winter of her soul, Cattie had suffered several unspeakable tragedies. But she stood to her feet and, still stalwart in her stand for her Lord, made her own "three-pointer." Heaven is still cheering.

The beautiful day came to a close while the ocean rolled over the sandy shore and the sun quietly slipped behind it.

What grace!

6

Garbage Day

Winter was coming. I had to close the vents and cover the water faucets. I also had to roll up the garden hoses and put them in the shed.

With my jogging suit on I pulled on gloves and started the hose business. After emptying the water from them, I pulled and tugged to get the hoses rolled up. It looked so easy when Harold did it, and he always got them neatly tied up and hung in the shed.

Now I stood there, all tangled up in the twisted hoses. I finally piled them up, in total disarray, on the wheelbarrow in the shed.

Tears streamed down my face; I lashed out at the mess. "I hate those stupid hoses—and all those tools. I don't know what to do with them. How can I ever make it alone?"

"What's the matter, Margaret?"

I turned into the loving embrace of one of our "adopted" children, Bob Hoffman. "I hate those hoses!"

Then we both laughed. Somehow love has a way of bringing soothing oil into the frictions of life.

"I miss him too; it's like losing my dad. But you'll make it! Let us all help."

Bob and Mary Jane had been caught in some twisted hoses of life, leaving security on the West Coast, moving cross-country to the East, and then losing a promised job when they got there. After that, they weathered one trouble after another, and nothing seemed to make sense. Yet in all the twisting and turning, one thing remained unchanged: their faith in a loving God.

> On Christ, the solid Rock, I stand;
> All other ground is sinking sand.[1]

With love and prayer Bob made his way home to Florida in the midst of the twisted hoses that seemed to be unnecessary tangles of life.

Faith was still intact!

I read where faith is secured by adversity, but endangered by security. To me it seemed that a little security really wouldn't hurt my faith any, especially on this cold, rainy morning. Besides, it was garbage day!

I could see Harold with his usual good humor making a mock bow. "I have an announcement to make, Mrs. Jensen. *It is garbage day!*" With a flourish he gathered the trash and rolled the garbage can down the driveway. Mission accomplished, he got the paper and we enjoyed our coffee and news, but mostly Dennis the Menace.

Now I sometimes forget garbage day, but today I remembered. This day I would remember for a long time—wet, cold, rainy, and an overflowing can.

Someone had sent a beautiful card with a note: "God has great plans for you, good plans."

I pulled the can down the driveway in the rain. "Some plan," I muttered. "Couldn't You come up with a better plan, Lord? Garbage cans in the rain? And heavy at that."

The newspaper was wet and my coffee was cold. "I think I could have come up with a better plan than this. Why take Harold when I need him so much?" I made another pot of coffee, changed my wet jogging suit, and turned up the heat.

Well, at least I made it this time. I could hear the familiar chime of the garbage truck. Believe me, that monstrous can will stay at the end of the driveway until it stops raining. So much for this garbage day!

The coffee was good. I was warm and the newspaper had dried. Dennis brought a chuckle.

I was reminded for a moment about when Jesus was up on the mountain of transfiguration. The disciples were thrilled to be with Him. "Oh, let's just stay here," they said.

"Sorry, gentlemen, but today is garbage day— down in the valley of human need." Garbage day! The newspaper was full of it: human need, sorrow and sin, a world without God.

"I have great plans for you."

"Lord, can it be You need me for garbage day?"

Oh, no, not a garbage collector?

Well, maybe.

7

The Peaceable Kingdom

During September and October, 1991, I had traveled through nine states and spoken twenty-eight times. On the last trip Harold took me to the airport. I was headed for Oregon, but I was reluctant to leave. The airport attendant jokingly said, "You are running late today," which was unusual for us. Harold was always early.

"I just don't want to leave. I like being home with this man."

Quietly Harold put his arm around me. "Margaret, you are one of a kind, a unique storyteller who communicates God's love so all can understand. I know that. When the doors open, you go, and I'm always with you."

That was the last time he sent me out to tell the story of Jesus and His love. October 31, 1991, Harold boarded a chariot and went Home.

The next time I boarded a plane was in January of 1992. It was my first time to speak after Harold had left me. I went alone—or was I alone? "Lo, I am with you always."

That time I was headed for the New England Congress of Evangelism in Boston, Massachusetts, to be held on January 31, and a visit to Gordon College where I would speak.

It was good to be with Jan and Jud and see the grandchildren. I watched Shawn, a freshman at Gordon, play basketball. I attended a play where Chad was the hero. Heather and her friend, Kris Wood, sang in a gospel chorus. They were all at the college, a part of the student body. My offer to adopt any student brought lines of applications, so I really can't count my "grandchildren." My "children" came from around the world and I wanted to hold them all and protect them from a world that is not very peaceable.

I was reminded how the kingdom of God is within us. Peace and joy are not found in external places, but within a heart surrendered to God.

Tourists crowd the streets of quaint towns to sample the quiet, gentle ways of a long-ago day, and then they return to the frenzy of TV dinners and hectic schedules. Perhaps that is what Harold meant, that the stories of faith from the yesterdays bring us back to the peaceful kingdom within. The old paths, the old ways, should not be forgotten, but the children of God can move like a river of life in the midst of a restless, modern world.

Looking at my favorite audience, college youth, I realized I could not hold them in spite of adopting them, but I could share the stories of faith to rekindle their hopes for tomorrow. My heart cried out, "Take the old path, two thousand years old! It is still the only road to the peaceful kingdom within. Jesus is the Way, the Truth, and the Life. No one comes to the Father but by the old way, Jesus Christ."

Then to the Congress—it was awesome! Six thousand people from New England gathered in the Hynes Auditorium in Boston. Our daughter, Jan Carlberg, and Charlie Austin (the golden voice of Boston) were, by popular request, the master of ceremonies—they were the audience's favorites. Their combination of wit and sensitivity made even announcements exciting.

The general theme of the Congress was, "I Have Engraved You in the Palm of My Hand" (see Isaiah 49:16).

Phillip Yancey gripped our hearts with the age-old question, "Where is God when it hurts?"

Jack Hayford reminded us that the shout of joy brings fruit out of barrenness (Isaiah 54).

Luis Palau's "Just Do It" message brought a new challenge to some of us who wait for the "right time" and allow molten moments to slip away.

Jan and I did a workshop on the "Generation Grasp" that brought the old stories of faith from generation to generation into our modern culture.

Several months earlier, Harold had watched me record my notes from an open Bible for the theme given to me, "I Will Not Forget You." He was looking forward to going with me to Boston.

It had been easy to write those notes when loved by family and friends, and supported and encouraged by Harold. But when the winter of the soul came, for a moment I felt forgotten. "God, where are You?"

Now I suddenly felt very alone. Who was I to bring a message to New England?

Then I remembered!

I was not a tourist walking the quaint streets of a peaceful town. I was a pilgrim who has learned to trust the old path—the one way, the God who was the Creator of heaven and earth.

Spurgeon said that hell and its fury is no match against the Creator of heaven and earth. This was the God into whose hand I was engraved.

I also remembered a long-ago time when there was a cry from Calvary, "Oh, God, not You! Everyone else has turned away, but not You, My Father. Don't leave Me!"

For a moment God did turn away. And the price was paid! "It is finished" has come echoing through the corridors of time.

God turned away from the sin of the world for a moment, but He knew Easter was coming. He knew that the atonement was the fulcrum upon which time and eternity turned.

"He is alive!" burst into history, and humanity could be reconciled to God through Jesus Christ His Son. *No one need be left alone!*

I tucked away my notes, for out of my heart came the message, "I Will Not Forget You."

In the winter of the soul, God remembered me, and I know He will not forget you.

A few weeks later, I flew to Amana, Iowa, the epitome of peaceful, a town with quaint streets. When I arrived, the town was dressed in the grey of winter, showed a faint hue of green, hope for the coming of spring. Pictures of summer flowers confirmed that out of spring bursts a fairyland of color—hope!

The women still quietly tied their black aprons on, wrapped black shawls around their shoulders, and fastened their black bonnets.

They came, heels clicking on the wooden floor, and they sat together, row by row, on the wooden benches.

The men filed in through another door and also took their places row by row, separate from the women.

Three elders faced the hushed congregation, and the service began. Old hymns were sung *a capella* and we knelt on wooden benches to pray. No one stirred as we listened to a rather lengthy reading of Scriptures. Then, as quietly as they came, so they left. Reverence for God and His church was a deeply ingrained way of life for these gracious people.

At the same time, the streets were filled with the tourists. In the long-ago past, communal kitchens had kept families eating together; today, restaurants flourish while happy visitors enjoy the famous German dishes.

Gentle Melissa had planned a Spring Festival Luncheon for the entire community, and I, the guest speaker, had come from the outside world. The people readily opened their homes and hearts to this "outsider."

The beautiful children, home schooled during the week, gathered on Sunday to learn Bible verses and hear the stories about biblical heroes. I wondered how long this secluded work of peace and contentment could last.

The Amana story began in Germany in 1714. Due to persecution, the Amana society eventually settled in Iowa where seven villages developed, known as the

Amana Colonies. In 1932 the communal lifestyle was restructured along corporate lines, and today it is a thriving, unique enterprise.

At the meeting house I viewed videos of past history, then toured the furniture factory, woolen mill, bakery, and smokehouses. The hanging Amana quilts, tapestries of art, held me spellbound. In our present day of disposable plastic, how refreshing to see the unique blending of old-world craftsmanship and strong work ethic with the efficiency of the twentieth century business world.

Too soon, the time came to leave Amana. While I sat in the airport waiting for my flight to North Carolina, I tucked the memories of these gentle people into the recesses of my mind.

In my suitcase I carried some freshly baked bread and apricot coffeecake, gifts from this peaceable kingdom in Amana.

The sounds and scents of the shops and restaurants teeming with happy families would linger in my memory for many days.

It seems to me that sometimes the outside world longs to take a tour into the past, perhaps to renew their courage to face the stresses of their tomorrows.

The admonition from the old prophet Jeremiah (6:16) was a reminder to "stand ye in the ways, and see, and ask for the old paths, where is the good way, and walk therein, and ye shall find rest for your souls."

Weariness had engulfed me as I thought of the long flight ahead—the three-hour layover in Kansas City, then to Charlotte, and finally the last leg home on the late flight.

For the first time Harold would not be there, but I would not be forgotten. Ralph, our son, would be there. And so would my Father.

While the plane flew across the miles I allowed the rest from the peaceable kingdom to steal into my restless places and prayed for the wisdom to choose the good paths.

When traveling and speaking, I sense the peace that comes from being in God's will. I owe Harold much. Because of his unselfish love and encouragement I can continue alone; yet, I never really feel alone. His presence stays with me like the wind beneath my wings.

P.S. Weeks passed. One day a large package arrived. It held a beautiful Amana quilt and a picture of the gentle people putting endless stitches into a work of art.

The tiny stitches said, "You are loved and we didn't forget you."

Isn't that what God keeps telling us?

8

Just Checking

After our New Year's Eve dinner in 1980, I passed out paper and pens with the suggestion that we each write down our desires for the coming year. The envelopes were sealed and placed in my desk drawer, and then forgotten.

We went on with our lives. Earlier our family had begun to build a beautiful dream in Greensboro, but circumstances prevented its completion. Then Harold was encouraged to build his own dream in Wilmington. I came "kicking and screaming," reluctant to leave my safe place in Greensboro.

"But Doris," I complained to my sister, "you know Harold's decisions aren't always wise—this is ridiculous!"

"You owe it to Harold to trust the God in him; forget past mistakes, and trust in God's leading Harold."

I did! (Thank you, Doris.)

It was the best move we ever made. The later years were greater than the former. Harold urged me to write.

"For forty years Margaret supported me in every venture; now it is my turn to help her fulfill her dream," he told a publisher. And he did! He typed, edited, made travel arrangements, helped with mail, and drove on endless errands to keep me free to write. I wrote in longhand, and Harold prayed for the gift of interpretation when he transferred my yellow pages to the typewriter.

It was Harold who always made the office ready for writing. We drank our coffee and read the newspaper in the kitchen while the office "got ready."

"It's warm now, Margaret; you can go out and write."

In the summer he turned on the air. "It's cool now; you can write."

We did eight books together.

But now he was gone and my beautiful office lay silent for several months. I wondered if I would ever write again.

Soon after Harold died I sent out seven hundred pieces of mail, all written, not in my office, but in the dining room where I was near the happy faces on the wall. I felt safe there; the office was too lonely.

Finally, knowing I had to do it, one spring morning in 1992 I went to my office to clean out my desk. I found the New Year's Eve envelopes that had been put there eleven years before.

I opened Harold's.

He had written three desires, and I realized they all had been met, but not in one year:

1. He desired to see my first book, *First We Have Coffee*, published. Here's Life Publishers launched it in 1983.

2. He longed to see Ralph build his own shop in an industrial park. For days, weeks, and months, Harold drove around the area looking for building sites. Ralph and Chris finally made the decision—Dutch Square, on Old Dairy Road, off Market Street. Over Dunkin' Donuts they dreamed and planned; then on October 30, 1991, it was completed. Harold spent most of the day with Ralph watching each detail completed. They rejoiced together over a dream fulfilled. "He built dreams for others," Ralph said, "even when his own died." Harold viewed Ralph's dream and it was good. The next day, October 31, 1991, Harold went Home.

3. There was one more dream he saw fulfilled: Jan's book, *The Hungry Heart*, a devotional from the Old Testament, was completed. I remember how he wept when he read the manuscript. "The Holy Spirit has given Jan an insight into God's Work, and in her creative way she brings those words to linger in your heart." He held the finished book in his hand; through tears he read:

This book is for you, from my thankful heart for your choices to follow Jesus and your example and encouragement for me to do the same. May the God of the Old Testament feed your hungry hearts with all you long for and need for real life.

> I love you . . .
> Janice Dawn
> March 27, 1991

Our times are in God's hands, and sometimes He seems to wind the clock slowly. Eleven years—and the dreams were all fulfilled. God is never late!

That morning the hours flew by, and then a familiar step announced it was time for lunch. "Come on," Chris said, "let's go to Swensens'! You need a break." So, we went!

When I left the office, I quietly closed the door. Writing would come later. Now was time for lunch with Chris and Ralph. We laughed; we talked; and we made happy plans together.

Then I decided this afternoon would be garden time.

Ralph found a yardman to help with the garden chores. Buddy tilled the garden, trimmed the shrubbery, raked endless leaves, and told me what I needed: lime, fertilizer and grass seed.

We worked together in the warm spring sunshine and his country humor kept me entertained. "Yep! We had revival in our little country church! Yes, sir! We had revival! Could he preach! Oh, Lordy, could he preach! Yes, sir, he could preach!"

"What did he preach about?"

"I'll tell you he could preach. Preached agin' long hair and earrings; yes, sir, them earrings and long hair."

Buddy watched me plant my beans and shook his head. "How you gonna get straight rows without marking with string?"

"Oh, Buddy, I don't worry about straight rows. Just wait until the garden comes up and then I'll know what I planted."

Buddy scratched his head. "No way to plant a garden, no way a'tall!"

A friend of Buddy's came to check our patio plan. "We had revival at our church. Yes, sir, revival. Some folks, though, didn't go to the altar and they need to! Heard tell some don't even tithe. No way you git saved effen you don't tithe. Yes, sir, a dime out of each dollar. Some folks sure need to go to the altar."

Sometimes Buddy and I would take a break in the afternoon, with cold milk and cookies. "Don't mind if I do. Yes, sir, don't mind if I do."

One hot afternoon I sat in the patio swing watching my neighbor rake leaves. Suddenly I was crying my eyes out. Harold won't be here to rake leaves.

Then I looked up into the sky. "Harold Jensen, I don't know why I'm bawling my eyes out. You never did rake the leaves—Shawn and I did it!"

I called Jan. "It was so funny, Jan; there I was crying, and then I'm laughing. That's not all. I told Uncle Jack [Harold's brother] how I missed Harold, and he just said, 'Well, you can count on it—he doesn't miss us.'" We both had a good laugh.

"Well, Jan, now our Buddy is hitting on a new project—cutting down the pampas grass. 'Much too high,' he says, 'yes, sir, much too high. How come you don't watch soap operas? All the women I do yard work for watch soap operas. How come you work all the time?' He shook his head and kept cutting the pampas grass."

Jan abruptly changed the subject. "Mother, be sure you keep your doctors' appointments. Get your eyes checked, also your hearing. You aren't hearing too well. And don't forget the dentist."

I made the list: Dr. Fulk—ears okay. ("I'm not deaf, just ignoring you.") Dr. Poole—eyes okay. (Not bad when I read the newspaper without glasses. Why all the fuss?) Dr. Hutchen—okay. Dr. Mason—okay. Dr. Wells—okay. (I do have a corn, but it's not fatal!)

At first it seemed Jan was unnecessarily checking, but then I realized she was expressing her fear that something could happen to me. That would be another loss, and she couldn't have handled that. Yet I know that my times were in God's hands. He winds the clock.

The garden is up now! Poor Buddy can't figure out how the beans grew into a straight row. Tomato plants are okay. The rabbits got the cabbages and did a number on the lettuce. I plant too much anyhow.

I planted flowers all over the place because I wanted everything the same, just like Daddy did it, for when the children come.

When Shawn comes from Gordon, the boys can wash the windows. Harold forgot the two back windows last year.

> I'm making a list,
> Checking it twice
> The garden and house
> Must be nice.

The children are coming!
I wondered, "How does it look from heaven?" If Harold is checking, I'm sure he is smiling.

9

The Ultimate Frisbees

In March 1992, I flew in from Chicago and Jan came in from California in time to meet the Ultimate Frisbee Team from Gordon College, coming to compete in the University of North Carolina, Wilmington, tournament.

Fifteen Frisbee players arrived in a large van, which had "Bullriders, South to Wilmington, N.C." painted in huge letters all over it. The players spilled out with sleeping bags and surfboards, and a large sign for the garage.

Thanks to the creative genius of number one grandson, Chad Carlberg, the neighbors were well informed.

And we were ready! We opened cots, unrolled foam mattresses, and ended up with wall-to-wall Frisbee players in my office, den, and garage. Early in the morning I even stumbled over two bodies wrapped in bedspreads on the living room floor. Chad was in his ultimate glory—his friends were in North Carolina for the tournament during spring break.

While the team tossed Frisbees in the backyard, played horseshoes, or headed for the beach, Jan, Chris, and I kept the stove hot, cooking for our hungry crowd.

The newspaper reporters came for interviews and stayed for supper. The washer and dryer drew overtime while the dishwasher endured continuous active duty.

Chad was aware of the empty place left by the absence of his beloved Papa. "If my Papa were here, we'd listen to all his old jokes, get a Chamber of Commerce tour of Wilmington, and go to a Southern breakfast at the White Front—sausage, grits, eggs and biscuits."

We all missed Harold's warm presence, but I have an idea he had the angels cheering for "the ultimate Frisbee players." The competition was keen, and, though they didn't win, our Gordon players did extremely well.

One night we took them to Jackson's where the team was introduced to Southern barbecue, corn bread and peach cobbler. The marquee at Jackson's announced to the world: "Welcome Gordon College Frisbee Team."

Friday came and I had to take the 7A.M. flight to California. Jan and Chris stayed to see the happy team off the same day as they headed back to classes. Today, pictures on my wall prompt memories of the happy sounds of youth at play.

"We cleaned up, Grammy." And they did!

"Y'all come back!"

Jan returned to Washington, D.C., to speak at a retreat for the women of Fourth Presbyterian Church, and I went to the West Coast for two retreats, one in Irvine, California, at the Marriott, and the other the next weekend in La Jolla.

Between those weekends I visited my lifelong friend, Rose, and saw my Here's Life publishing family. On Wednesday I enjoyed a great day with Scott and Ann Hilborn and their church family at Canoga Park. God has His nails in sure places (see Isaiah 22:23) all across the land.

On Thursday, in Irvine, I had my own ultimate experience—no voice! In a beautiful pink setting for a banquet, five hundred women were expecting their guest speaker—me—and I had no voice!

Just in case of such an emergency I had brought a tape with me and tried to give it to the leaders. "We won't need it," they said. I kept trying to give it to them and they wouldn't take it. Instead they prayed! And so did I!

While the happy crowd sang songs of faith and joy, I put my head in my hands. (They thought I was praying, but I was crying.) *If only Harold were here, this wouldn't be happening.* I wanted him to pick me up in his arms and carry me home. Self-pity engulfed me while everyone else was singing. I had never felt so helpless and alone.

"Why, God? Isn't it enough to travel without Harold? Now am I to be humiliated before this audience? If only I could run away and hide. The guest speaker—and no voice!"

Was God really in charge? Had He allowed this humiliation for a purpose? Why was I here?

I wanted to go home—home, where I was safe and loved and care for. Chris would be there to fix spice-tea. Ralph would pray peace into my troubled spirit. And I wanted my own pillow.

Spiritual warfare became real to me that night, and while everyone else sang I was caught in a battle. This was not the ultimate Frisbee team; this was the ultimate spiritual battle.

Would I go down in self-pity? Or could I rise to acknowledge the sovereignty of God and His promise to work good out of this—my having no voice?

I yielded to Him. "Lord, forgive my self-pity, and I surrender to Your will." As I prayed, I began to realize in a new way that God doesn't need my voice to speak to His people. (He even used a donkey once.)

I heard God's still voice: "Trust Me."

It was then I heard the leader announce the speaker of the evening, Margaret Jensen. Hers was the voice of faith.

When I walked up to the platform I whispered to Jesus, "Okay, it's just You and me. Do it Your way."

I whispered into a turned-up microphone, "I feel like Moses at the Red Sea and I'm not sure the waters will part. This will be a meeting no one will ever forget, and when we all get to heaven someone will say, 'Oh, I know you—the speaker without a voice.'"

Laughter rippled through the audience. Then it was quiet.

"God must have something very important to say to each of us tonight. If you are very quiet, you will hear the Holy Spirit speak to you—and you alone. God doesn't need me or my voice, but when He speaks, we must listen."

Steadily my voice increased and I was beginning to sound like Jimmy Durante. The hushed audience listened to me, and I listened to Him, the still small voice that said, "Trust Me." A gentle presence covered me with peace and I continued two full sessions. When it was over I couldn't even whisper.

Weeks later I was still receiving letters and calls telling me how many guests had been invited who were involved in the occult or the New Age, or who were without any church affiliation.

They listened to this strange speaker and somehow heard.

Someone said to me, "You can't imagine how many tapes were sold—to hear the Jimmy Durante voice."

Perhaps many came with skeptical and cynical minds, but they saw faith in action and knew it was real. God has His own way to speak to His children—and to me.

On Friday I arrived at the La Jolla retreat where I was met by a group of subdued leaders and speakers. They had voices just like mine!

With a sense of awe, Patsy, Marilyn, and I filed into the prayer room with Marita and the other leaders, the room where intercessory prayer was made for this retreat.

This was no frisbee game! It was real, a strange kind of warfare.

Songs of praise filled the ballroom, and when the musicians led the audience in "There Is Power in the Blood," we knew victory before we saw it. There were tears and laughter and a sense of God's presence as individual hearts heard God speak, through disabled voices.

"Not by might, nor by power, but by my spirit" (Zechariah 4:6) became a reality to speakers who were not used to feeling so helpless.

Long after I returned home, messages kept coming across the miles.

"We sensed God's presence in a new way."

"I've never been to a retreat like this one."

"My life was changed."

Out of apparent defeat, God had His victory. He had turned us all into His own "Ultimate Frisbees"!

Hurrah for the team!

10

The Letter

April 24, 1992

Dearest Jan,

I'm on the plane again!

Believe me, even the airport attendants were impressed with my new luggage. In fact, I miss my beat-up blue bag, taped and full of holes. After all, it had been to Europe and Nigeria—without me, of course.

I remember when Scott prayed, "Oh, Lord, we usually pray for lost people; today we pray for lost luggage to return safely home."

It did—with a few more holes, but nothing missing. Now Katie wants it.

My adopted children, Grace and Bob, saw my pitiful luggage and sent a new five-piece set for my birthday. How could they know how attached I had become to my world-traveling bag (with or without me)?

However, this beautiful blue luggage doesn't look like the wandering kind. Eric proudly carried my new bags to the car, and we will travel together with a new dignity and respect, I hope, and in style.

I had a wonderful break over Easter and enjoyed my seventy-sixth birthday with the family, but somehow I wasn't prepared for the effect Easter would have on me. Harold seemed to be all over the place—in the garden, at the communion service—and I found myself getting into the car on the passenger side.

Eric had stayed with me the entire week before Easter, working in the garden until it looked like a park.

Easter morning, for the children's annual Easter egg hunt, Eric hid the plastic, candy-filled Easter eggs in the bushes. Benjamin and Paul, my nephew's little boys, would also be there.

Last year, the dog found the Easter eggs.

I seemed to hear Harold in the shower and I knew he would come out smelling like Aqua-Velva and all dressed up. How he loved to dress up! I almost heard him singing "He Lives," and then I was brought into my all-alone world again. It was so quiet and empty.

I grabbed Eric—just heading for the car. "Where is your tie, young man?"

"Aw, Grammy, I hate ties. Besides, I forgot mine."

"Papa has a rack full."

He found a beautiful tie of Harold's, and a shadow crossed his face. I wanted to cry. Almost.

I missed Harold's special surprises, a beautiful hanging basket and cards. Oh, those beautiful cards he was famous for. Jan, do you remember how you said, "I can always tell a Daddy card"? (Didn't say much for my selection.)

The Easter service was glorious, but I cried on the inside. At one point I felt a long, bony arm around my shoulders and a quick hug. Eric, wearing Papa's tie, was saying without words, "You aren't alone, and Papa lives."

That's when I choked back the tears and sang with all the gusto faith could muster:

> He lives, He lives . . .
> I know He lives.
> He lives within my heart.

Christ and Harold within my heart. No wonder he seemed so close.

(We're on the runway now, waiting to take off.)

Suddenly I felt thanksgiving rise up. What an honor to represent the Lord Jesus, the Living One, to a world of people crying on the inside while laughing on the outside.

An exhilarating joy seemed to burst into my soul—He lives! This alive Jesus can bring forth life even through the death of dreams and a broken spirit.

"We've a story to tell to the nations" seemed to echo in my heart, and all of a sudden it was a joy to clean the bathrooms, finish the laundry, check the refrigerator, pack my bags, lay out my travel suit, and get up at 5 A.M. to catch the 7 A.M. flight. I even had my carry-on bag filled with books to give to the plane crew—my away-from-home family.

You should have seen Eric! Believe it or not, I just called him once at 5 A.M. and there he stood, in his baseball uniform, ready to carry out my new bags.

We swallowed a cup of coffee and took off. I saw Harold in that tall young man—all legs and arms—and I didn't hurt so much inside. "He lives."

"*I'll pick you up, Grammy, don't worry about anything. I have my list of chores.*" He looked so young and vulnerable.

Landing! Indianapolis! "*Praise God, from whom all blessings flow.*"

I'm having a good day.

Love,
Mother

11

The Marker

Ralph and Chris went with me to visit the grave.
The cemetery was alive with flowers from Easter.
Harold's grave was bare.
A bronze marker had just been placed there and the
soil was still waiting for the grass to grow.
I couldn't believe his body was there—tie and all!

HAROLD EDWARD JENSEN
1912–1991

Then I saw:

MARGARET TWETEN
1916–

I wondered why my last name wasn't there, then
forgot about that as I began to wonder how much time
I had.

I recalled a day, long before that second marker was etched in bronze, when I had felt the pressures of writing and travel smothering me. I kept thinking, *Time is so short, and I have "miles to go before I sleep."*[1]

Panic set in. *Borrowed time—I'm on borrowed time!*

Quietly a woman of God had reached out to me. "You will have all the time you need for God to accomplish His purpose through you, and there is much He has given you to do." Peace settled in like a gentle stream.

God had His marker for me before I was even born, not in bronze but in the nail prints in His hands. I was safe!

Many years ago in a Youth for Christ rally I sang with all the fervor of youth about being safe and sheltered in the hand of the Lord.

Sixty years later I knew the meaning: "My times are in thy hand" (Psalm 31:15). God winds the clock.

I'm looking now out of a plane window and I see billows of clouds lined up in a row over a sea of glass. Where is heaven? I keep looking into the clouds and wishing I could somehow see the city filled with loved ones, and maybe see Harold waving to me. Sometimes I even say, "Good morning, heaven, wherever you are."

I wish God would open the gates and let me peek, but I'm not sure I would want to stay here then. Maybe I wouldn't be willing to get up at 5 A.M. to catch the 7 A.M. flight. Maybe the stories I had to tell to the nations would not seem so urgent.

So I just tell the clouds, "Go ahead and hide your city. I happen to know it's there because Jesus said He went to prepare a place, and when the time is right He will send for me."

When the grandchildren were young I would tell them that when we got to heaven we'd slide down the white clouds as though they were slippery marshmallows, and we'd play tag.

When Katie was very young she used to say, "I know what Bestemör [my mother] is doing. She's sitting in a rocking chair telling stories to the children in heaven. I will be so happy to go there."

Heaven is real! Beautiful! Happy! A child's faith! We all need it.

When ten-year-old Timothy Tepper died in a car accident, Katie grieved for her "forever friend." When her beloved Papa died, the tears fell when she grieved alone in the restroom at school.

"Grammy, I miss Papa so much, but then the peace of God comes all over me. Now Timothy knows someone in heaven and Papa is holding his hand and taking him all over the place. You know Papa—he had to shake hands with everyone. Now he takes Timothy with him."

That settled it! Faith sees what the eye can never see. Eye hasn't seen nor has ear heard what God has prepared for His people. Children come the closest to seeing and hearing.

Why is it so difficult for us to become like little children? Why do we need all the answers? Somehow the ego in us thinks we have a right to know God's ways. But God tells us that His ways and thoughts are not our ways and thoughts (see Isaiah 55:8).

The awesome silence of God thunders louder than all our screaming questions. Across the corridors of time comes the answer: "Be still, and know that I am God" (Psalm 46:10).

Then the tears come and wash into the deep, hardened crevices of the stony place in my heart. Gently, ever so gently, the Spirit of God plants flowers of faith: "I've come this far by faith" and "I've come too far to turn back now."

I saw the jostling crowds with a new compassion, and I wondered how many broken hearts would harden because they didn't know the God of comfort. I had a story to tell.

P.S. The flowers are on the grave now—beautiful yellow daffodils that remind us of spring and resurrection. The grass is coming through the sandy soil. We know he is not there, and it is a reminder to us. Our days soon fade, like grass and flowers, but we shall live forever in the presence of the King. We are engraved in the palm of His hand.

12

No Tuna Fish Tonight

The sun slowly sank and the woods in the back of the house looked dark and mysterious.

Number three grandson, Eric, had manicured the lawn to look like a park. In the yard, azaleas in full bloom dominated the scene and brilliant red, soft pink, and lavender vied for attention. Around the edges, red salvia and yellow marigolds stood at attention.

Two doves, sitting on the edge of the patio roof, decided to take a dip in the birdbath. They are always together—kind of like Harold and me in the yester-days.

"Come on, Margaret," he would say, "let's take a look at the garden."

We'd tour the fairyland together, pluck a weed here and there, watch for new buds, check the palm trees and pampas grass. We admired the desert gold iris from Grandma Jensen's garden, fifty years ago. I could almost hear her chuckle. "I paid seventeen dollars for these bulbs."

Fifty years later those bulbs had been transplanted from garden to garden. Memories of loved ones never die.

Now I could almost hear Harold say, "Remember when we came to this house fourteen years ago?" I remembered how I cried when we left our lovely Greensboro home with its roses and azaleas to come to this barren place.

The yard here was a disaster—no grass, only weeds and prickly sandburs. There were no flowers, just some scraggly bushes, and we dug them up.

I recalled crying in the rain while I planted forty yucca bushes beside the college road. Together Harold and I rolled wheelbarrows of sand to fill the sunken hollow by the dead-end road, and then we planted holly bushes, azaleas, and monkey grass.

We found rocks from deserted lots and filled the sliding banks with them. Orange lilies now thrive between the rocks.

One day a truck pulled up with ten palm trees.

"Oh, no," I cried, "you must have the wrong house."

"Nope! Got the right house. That's exactly what your husband told us you would say."

Throughout the years, when others played golf, Harold planted gardens. He tilled the ground and planted vegetables, and then he planted flowers and fruit trees. His motto was, "Always leave a place more beautiful than when you found it."

He did!

It was getting dark outside now and I had to close the blinds on the bay window and turn on the lights. That's the hardest part of the day. I don't like to close the blinds because it seems that Harold is out in the yard, watering the flowers around the corner, and I'm shutting him out.

I forgot to water the window box again. Poor Uncle Jack, Harold's eighty-five-year-old brother, shakes his head as only a sorrowful gardener can do. "Margaret, the window box doesn't get rain and those expensive plants will die."

So . . . I watered the window box before I closed the blinds.

That's not all I forgot. The garbage can! Harold never forgot the window box or the garbage can.

One thing I did know. I was not eating tuna fish tonight. No way!

I did that last night when I sat in the breakfast nook and watched the rain splash against my bay window. Harold and I used to enjoy sitting in the shadows of the evening, watching the rain. We loved it when we saw the garden soak up the water of life.

"No need to cook tonight, Margaret, let's just have a tuna fish sandwich and a cup of hot tea and watch the rain."

It was raining last night so I fixed a tuna fish sandwich and watched the rain, alone. I choked on it. The potato chips were stale; the tea was cold. Only my tears were hot. I closed the blinds and turned on all the lights. The winter of the soul had set in and the rain cried with me.

That was last night. Tonight I said, "No tuna fish."

The soon-to-be baked potato found a home in the microwave while I prepared a small steak and salad, tea, and a cookie.

Katie's ball game kept me cheering earlier; then grocery shopping occupied my time because the next day was Mother's Day.

I wanted Chris, my angel daughter-in-law, to have a break—she always prepares the traditional Sunday dinner when I travel. But now I was home and it was my turn to cook Sunday dinner.

After my supper, I checked my list.

While the angel food cake rose majestically in the oven, I set the table for Sunday dinner. Fresh strawberries and real whipped cream, Sarah's favorite dessert.

I checked corn on the cob, Katie's favorite, to go with the family's choice of roast beef, mashed potatoes, green beans, and applesauce.

I made one big decision: no more watching the rain alone, and no tuna fish. It was much better to plan a meal for a family of hungry, happy people.

I'll miss Harold's cards and hanging baskets for Mother's Day. I could certainly remember to buy hanging baskets, but it's not the same.

Oh well, I'll do that next week; the patio does look lonely without the flowers. But I can't remember everything! One thing I will remember—no more tuna fish on a rainy night. I'll call the "gang" for pizza!

Somehow I'd make it through another holiday. I checked my list again, and it was time to go to bed. I turned out the lights while the grandfather clock said good night eleven times.

When the clock announced a new day with six chimes, I knew it was time to put the roast in the oven. I stripped the corn, snapped the beans, cut up the strawberries, and peeled the potatoes. I was off to a running start. But it was another holiday without

Harold, and the lonesome song began coming on, so I determined to do the day up right.

I dressed in a white suit and purple blouse and slipped into my wild purple and cranberry shoes. After I checked the roast and turned off the oven I headed for the door, dangling my keys and swinging my purple straw bag. Just as I locked the door, there stood my handsome men, Ralph and Eric.

"No way my gorgeous mother is going to church alone."

Bowing, Eric opened the car door with a flourish, and we were off to church.

Poor Chris, mother of four, would have to make it in the weather-beaten jeep. God is surely mounting jewels for her crown.

I was greeted with, "Wow! Travel agrees with you." I chuckled to myself. Harold would like that. Sharp clothes suited him.

The grandchildren gave me that "you are cool" look and I knew the tears on the inside didn't show. Hurrah for this team!

Chris turned to me and whispered, "Well, Grammy, you did it again—purple and white!"

I whispered back, "I didn't want to look like a grieving widow."

"Well, you don't have to look like such a happy widow."

That's when we laughed out loud.

When Sunday dinner was a treasured memory, I read the beautiful cards again. "You are loved; you are loved; you are loved," appeared over and over.

A Lizzie Hill doll from Jan and Jud sat on the buffet. From a long-ago past, the wooden Miss Hattie, with her basket of ironing, stood beside an ironing board holding an old iron. It was a reminder of one of my stories from *First We Have Coffee*.

I was fourteen and complained to my mother about how tragic life could be. The boy I liked had a crush on my girlfriend and she, in turn, liked someone else.

"Oh, Mama, life is so mixed up I could die."

"Oh, ja," Mama answered in her soft Norwegian accent, "but while you are dying, iron!"

She pulled out the basket of starched clothes from under the kitchen table, and I ironed until I gave up on the idea of dying; besides, Mama had meatballs for supper and I was hungry.

This was a story I shared across the miles: "Don't just sit in despair. Do something! Iron!"

Today the story came back to me: "Don't cry in the rain and eat tuna fish. Call the gang for pizza."

I looked out the breakfast window. There on the patio Ralph had hung three beautiful flowering baskets.

I think I hear Harold cheering.

13

The Altered Suit

"'Mrs. Chisholm, do you think you can alter Papa's suit to fit me?'

"There he stood, Margaret, all six feet five inches of him, holding Harold Jensen's suit over his arm. His sad face held unshed tears when he held out the suit. I wanted to cry, but I said, 'Of course, Shawn, I can fix your Papa's suit for you.'

"'I want to wear Papa's suit'—we understood each other and talked for hours. We had the same heart for God."

And so it came to pass that number two grandson walked into church and filled Papa's place in the pew.

He wore Harold's grey suit, white shirt, and red tie, and even his socks and shoes. For a moment I saw Harold at nineteen, too serious for one so young, so tall, and so thin.

I wondered what the future held for this number two grandson.

Gloria Chisholm, my friend, had built a thriving laundry, dry cleaning, and dressmaking business with her husband, John, in the heart of the tumble-down inner city.

In 1984 I needed a certain color dress for a TV show in Atlanta. Frantically I glanced through the local Ad-Pak and noticed "dressmaking." That's when I met Gloria who became, as Sarah would say, "a forever friend." Gloria and I have been plotting and planning, cutting and sewing, ever since that day.

At one point I said to her, "Oh, Gloria, I'm going to be with the fabulous Florence in California and you have to think of something. She is gorgeous in her designer clothes."

"Now, don't you worry about that Florence-baby. We'll just take care of our Margaret-baby." And she did!

Then, in 1988, it was our fiftieth wedding anniversary, and Sarah and Kathryn were convinced the celebration was for them. "We want dresses that swish." They swished!

Harold used to pop in just to say hello to the Chisholms. "I love those special people—God's nails in a sure place. They are lights in a dark corner." Then Harold was gone.

Their love encircled me, and John said, "I can fix anything—just call me."

Gloria made the Norwegian outfit for Sarah who was invited to go with me and be a part of Scandia Day in Gig Harbor, Washington. Inez Glass's generous invitation made the special trip possible.

We stayed with the Nelsons, our "home in the West," and visited the Needle, the Nordic Historic

Museum, and the harbor, and we watched the gala 17th of May Parade when the community celebrated their Scandinavian Independence Day. While we were there, we also attended three different churches.

In 1984 the Nelsons and Inez Glass took me into their hearts and homes when, for the first time, I left Harold at home. I had never traveled alone, and the grandchildren wondered how I would ever make it to Seattle because I got lost in the parking lot at home. But I made it just fine.

When I came home, I said, "Harold, you must go with me next year. You will love them all!" He went, and he did! It turned out to be his favorite place and he was looking forward to another visit with his friend Eldred in 1992.

Harold went Home instead. Now Sarah was my companion on another flight without him. She helped Victoria Nelson manage the book table, and she also met the Nelsons' youngest daughter, Starla, a violin student who had been studying at the New England Conservatory of Music.

Finally, we were on our way home. The Norwegian outfit was packed in a suitcase for Kathryn. I plan to take her with me for another Scandia Day and she can wear it then.

Chad, Shawn, and Eric will probably go through Papa's jackets—they all want some part of him to hold on to.

Gloria will be there, needle in hand. "Of course I can alter these clothes."

Each of the children will carry a memory with an old paint shirt, a sweater, or a jacket. Even Sarah was looking for a shirt she could wear. Surely someone will want Papa's wild Hawaiian shirt—Katie, I expect.

We looked for Papa's treasures in a small chest and found pictures of his family, graduation announcements, a pocket knife, and some small coins. The pictures in the chest were the treasures of his heart.

We are the treasures of God's heart and He holds us in the palm of His hand. He clothes us in His Son's garment of righteousness.

And it needs no alterations!

14

The Choice

"Grammy, remember when Papa got all upset because we were playing cards? They were just fun cards."

"'Don't you ever play cards for money!'" Katie could imitate her Papa.

"When we asked him why he was so upset, he told us this."

It's a long story. I was only nineteen years old and it was during the Depression. I had a good job at the Bunte Candy Company in Chicago, but I had to quit school and go to work to help support my family.

I got in with some gamblers and learned to be good at cards. I was lucky, and I usually managed to have money when no one else had any.

One night, on a big winning streak, I was looking at the great cards in my hand and my pile of winnings in front of me. Then the strangest thing happened—I could hear my mother whisper in my ear, "The devil will take a finger, then a hand, and then he'll get you." Suddenly, I felt a battle raging within me. Money—money—win money! A gambling fever raged!

Then again, through the noise in the smoke-filled room, I heard a voice, "Get out! Leave now—or the devil will get you."

I jumped up, terrified of that burning lust for money and gambling I had just discovered within me. Shouting "Take it!" I pushed the winnings across the table, threw down the cards, and ran—ran from something controlling and evil.

Later I learned that a gang had come in and shot the men I sat with. Those were the infamous days of Al Capone. I never picked up another deck of cards because I knew how close I had come to becoming a compulsive gambler. I also realized how close I had come to being shot!

A little while after that, I went to the Humbolt Park Gospel Tabernacle, and there the message of God's love gripped my heart. I walked down the aisle to surrender my life to Jesus Christ.

How frightening to think that I could have been killed at that gambling table and never would have known the forgiveness of sin and God's amazing love.

"Just think, Grammy, we might never have known our Papa. That is some story!"

"That's not all," I added. "Papa was so happy to be a Christian that he spent hours reading the Bible and memorizing large portions of Scripture. He was only nineteen, yet he was asked to teach a large Sunday school class. Also, every night after work he went door-to-door telling people about Jesus.

"Your Papa's grandfather Mogenson was a Danish sea captain, and when he heard D. L. Moody preach, he opened his heart to receive Jesus Christ as his Savior. In return he established a mission in Denmark so seamen could hear the gospel.

"Papa's mother was listening to Dr. DeHaan on the radio when she knelt down by the radio to ask Jesus to be her Savior and Lord.

"When Papa became a Christian he attended evening classes at Moody Bible Institute. Years later I was able to tell stories on Prime Time America, on the Moody Station, with the host Jim Warren, one of the most talented, creative radio personalities around. It was an honor for me to be on his show.

"Who knows? Katie, maybe you will be next with all your creative stories. Jim and you could do a show and never miss a beat.

"With such a rich heritage, God expects much from all you children. Each of you has to make your own choice to receive God's gift of salvation. God's amazing grace is offered, but it is not inherited. To obey God is a personal choice. Papa made a choice many years ago, and because of that choice we are blessed. Just so, the generations to come will be blessed by the good choices you make."

"These days should be remembered and kept throughout every generation" (Esther 9:28).

15

Chad

"When are you coming, Chad?"

Believe me, there is no recession for the telephone company. Jan and I see to that.

"Not soon enough, Grammy, but I'm coming. How does my truck look?" Chad and another student were returning to reclaim his truck, sitting in my driveway.

"Beautiful! Shiny, like new!"

The poor truck, filled with happy Frisbee players, had collided with a Sears truck. No one was hurt, just their pride, but Chad's truck had been stranded in North Carolina for repairs.

Chad, number one grandson, is full of energy and creativity. One moment he is a hero in a play; the next he is off to China to study art. Between acts he manages to get the Gordon College Ultimate Frisbee team to come to North Carolina.

"Anything to see my Grammy."

That boy is a charmer, no doubt about it!

During a college banquet once, Chad dropped a stack of dishes while waiting on tables. There was a deafening crash, then silence, and Dr. Gross, the president, announced, "I want you to know that is Dr. Judson Carlberg's son." Chad, always the ham, jumped up on a chair and took a bow, and the disaster turned into a comedy.

When he was a young student in a play, he wouldn't allow the curtain to open until he was sure I was there. Jan said that face kept peeking between the curtains to see if I had arrived. When I did get there, I saw that young face with a grin from ear to ear peeking between the curtains, and the play began.

I've forgotten what the play was about, but I'll never forget the grin.

I see something of Harold in each grandchild: his creativity. His ability to dramatize biblical characters was so masterful that at one point every head turned when he said, "Here he comes!" He was acting out John the Baptist.

After World War II, when many broken hearts were grieving over lost loved ones, Harold designed and produced a Hollywood-type celebration to honor Gold Star mothers. It included choirs, bands, lights, color, and a golden flower for each of them. The sound of music, pomp, and pageantry added to the colorful crepe paper artwork dancing in the wind and brought joy to all who attended. The occasion was to honor one of the Gold Star mothers. It was a burst of creativity no one could forget, a molten moment; then the curtain closed and the lights went out.

Sometimes I see that burst of creativity in Chad, and I know that God winds the clock when our times are in His hands.

Out of our trial-and-error days will come a new understanding of God's ways and of His amazing grace to harness creativity, not to blow in the wind for just a moment, but to continue to move steadily by the fresh breeze of His Holy Spirit.

I'm glad Chad is coming, but I hurt when I know how much he will miss a Southern country breakfast with Papa.

I can cook all day, keep the oven hot with cakes and pies, but what does Chad remember? Biscuits at the White Front with Papa!

Papa's specialty was to take time with each child, and on the "I love Chad" day, he said, "Pick out any shirt, and don't look at the price tag."

He did! Don't try to get that surf-shop shirt away from Chad!

One of these days, before the Lord takes me Home, I expect to hear Chad preach a sermon the world won't forget, with the sound and fury, lights, action—and curtain!

Watch out world, the band is playing "Land of Hope and Glory" and the curtain is opening!

Chad, take a bow! Someone in heaven is applauding.

16

The Invader

The early dawn filtered through the grey skies with a gentle nudge to move me into a new day. Sleepily I stretched, arose, and went to the kitchen. With a yawn I reached for the coffeepot—then suddenly I was wide awake!

A cockroach had dared to invade my Norwegian kitchen!

One cockroach across the counter, and World War III was on! I put aside my Bible reading, and the newspaper could wait. Only the coffeepot stayed on course. Even my plans for writing came to a screeching halt while I tore into the cabinets. In my beat-up shorts and a red bandanna around my head, I slammed the contents of the shelves onto the table.

Then I saw the Wheatena box, and I had to stop a moment. I remembered a long-ago day when I had suggested to Harold, "Switch from oatmeal to Wheatena. It's good for you."

He agreed. One morning he brought a steaming bowl of Wheatena to me. "If it's good for me, it's good for you too."

Since I had grown up on oatmeal, which I did not like, my idea of breakfast did not include cooked cereal. But muttering a mock "thank you," I ate the Wheatena while Harold chuckled with delight.

Now he was gone, and I was crying again.

How ridiculous, I thought after a few minutes, *crying over a Wheatena box.* Memories are like that—they come stealing into your heart from the back roads of your mind and suddenly you cry, or laugh, or both.

I stopped crying and began laughing, "Okay, Harold, you win. Wheatena for breakfast—it's good for me." And I was back to the war on cockroaches!

The shelves received an unexpected scrubbing, and the fumigating was on.

The ring of the telephone brought me back to reality. "Yes, I could come to Seattle." I marked the date. "Just send a confirming letter. Oh, yes, I'm fine. Of course we all miss Harold more every day, but I stay very busy. I'm on the road too much, but I am trying to write."

I couldn't tell her about the Wheatena box; or that I laugh and cry at the same time. And I certainly couldn't say anything about scrubbing cabinets and chasing cockroaches. I was thankful she couldn't see me dressed for battle and armed with loaded spray guns.

Our conversation continued, then ended with a "God bless you," and I was back on the front lines of action.

During my disruptive day I thought about all the small things that come into everyday living. It's not only the great crises of life that break into our well-planned schedules, but also small things, like a cockroach in an orderly kitchen, that can create havoc.

Small frictions try men's souls, causing peace to take a detour and irritations to grate like rusty hinges. Grief makes us want to hide, or cry over a Wheatena box, but the cockroaches of life have a way of snapping us back to reality, and our perspective returns.

When I travel I prefer to sit by the window and hide behind a book or my yellow pad. I remembered a time when my quiet was invaded by a talkative woman spilling out trivialities, and uninvited irritation slipped into my peaceful world.

But suddenly, I was alert! A word, a phrase, and I heard a cry for help. My heart sorted through the trivia as her words spilled over like coffee into a saucer. In between the words, I heard the broken dreams, broken promises, and a broken heart. I closed my book and listened with my heart. Then we talked.

I reached into my weighted-down bag, overflowing with books, and found *Prop Up the Leanin' Side*.

Only God can "fix" things, but we can "prop up" along the way. Lena would have said, "Take them by the hand and tote them Home."

It was landing time and my friend carried her autographed book with her head a little higher and a smile playing around the corners of a weary face.

The cockroach brought my thoughts back to my kitchen and reality just as the phone rang again. It was Chris. "Mom, don't forget we meet at Swensens' for lunch today. Did you have a good morning? Hope you got lots of writing done."

"I'll tell you about my morning later." It's hard to explain about cockroaches over the phone. Somehow I seemed to know deep down in my heart that God does work out all these things for His good. But even cockroaches?

Well, I did get the upper cabinets clean, and the next day my eleven-year-old Katie would empty the lower cabinets.

She likes to crawl behind closed doors and spy out the land with a flashlight. To her it is like looking for dinosaurs in a dark cave, and an ant or a cockroach serves the same purpose. She attacks the corners with a Norwegian vengeance against dirt and bugs, then announces with triumph, "It's clear!"

My Norwegian Mama would be proud.

I put the spray guns away, closed the cabinets, and put the dishes in the dishwasher. Showered, dressed, and in my right mind, I eased my car into Swensens' parking lot. "How would you like to hear about my morning, Chris?"

I never gave her a chance to answer. Chris thought it was hilarious, so you see it wasn't such a bad day after all. A few tears, a good laugh, lunch at Swensens' —all are a part of living.

17

U.S. Air: 3-D

I looked up the aisle and thirteen-year-old Sarah, the princess, was wrapped in a blanket, sound asleep. This was her first flight across the wide blue yonder, and we were en route to Seattle, Washington. Since we couldn't get seats together, I asked the stewardess to check on that little girl of mine in 3-D.

Returning confused, the stewardess shook her head. There was no "little girl" in 3-D, only a beautiful young lady, five feet seven inches tall. Then she chuckled, "Grandmother." She could tell.

Only thirteen years ago that tiny baby sucked her thumb and refused to eat. Somewhere along the way that changed, and now it is one meal a day—all day long!

She looked the picture of innocence, soft brown hair curled around her face, just a baby!

I shuddered! The world around her, clamoring for her attention, would flash the bright lights and send the siren's call across the deep to lure her to an "island of dreams," where scorpions and serpents hide in the crevices of the rocks.

The monster, like an angel of light, would purr like a kitten. "Bow to me and you'll have your kingdom of dreams. Jump off the cliff of protective rules—no harm will come. Eat the stones I offer."

The music, the glamour, the lights are there, and the curtain opens. The stage is set. What part will she play?

In my mind I see a graduate in cap and gown, marching to the band sounds of "Land of Hope and Glory."

Life was a lot simpler for Harold and me; choices were black and white. Today too much grey can blur the vision. The basic values we grew up with were accepted by most of society: the sanctity of life; traditional family consisting of father, mother and children; Judeo-Christian ethics—all were considered the bedrock of society.

Now the fences are down! I feel guilty for allowing the social structure to change without a whimper from me—never a mumblin' sound. Now I am screaming, but there are too many voices, and who listens?

That little girl in 3-D, all curled up in a red blanket, doesn't have a clue as to what I'm ranting about on the inside. "Let the world go away. Get off my shoulder!" must have been my theme song while I nurtured my own family.

When Harold and I worked together to "rescue the perishing," we held our children close to us.

Since babysitters weren't in vogue, we planned our mini-vacations together: trips to the Jensen farm, picnics in forest preserves, and boat rides on the lake.

Since finances were usually below zero, we put a mattress for the children in the back seat and drove at night while it was cool. It was quiet and we could talk, that is until Janice, our number one child, opened her brown eyes at a "streak of dawn." "It's time to get up! It's morning!" It was 2 A.M. and the lights from the town were her streak of dawn.

We picnicked along the way while someone else dreamed the McDonald's dream.

During the years we tucked our children into bed, prayed and sang with them, while the world around us changed behind our backs.

Suddenly we were thrust into the arena of social change and we were almost destroyed as a family. The scars were not evident to the outside world but the wounds were deep.

Years passed before we realized how deep the wounds were in Harold's soul, a gentle, sensitive man. Perhaps that was why our beloved Papa held his grandchildren so close. "Let the world go away. Get off my shoulder," and he held his children's children under his protective arm, closer to his heart.

Now he watches from a box seat in the heavens while his little ones march to the "Land of Hope and Glory."

He also knows that we did what we could, and God honors faithfulness and the heart's love for Him.

I watch the little girl in 3-D, curled up under a red blanket, and I am reminded of how God covered our family, even with all our trials and errors, with the blanket of His love, grace and mercy. He will also cover our children's children.

The world won't go away; it keeps tapping on my shoulder, but faith hears the sound of God's approaching footsteps of salvation.

"I'll walk with you." "I won't leave you." "I'm with you." "My hands will turn the clock as you put your times into My hands" (see Psalm 31:15).

Landing time! It's been a long day and a missed connection added two extra hours of waiting. I don't want missed connections to God's ways to bring unnecessary delays in faith's journey.

Little girl in 3-D, it's time to rise up.

"Land of Hope and Glory." She's coming, world—watch out!

18

The Broken Branch

It's raining again! From my bay window I see the need for the yard work I had planned to do today—trim bushes, weed flower beds, transplant a red bush—but now it must wait.

I'll write instead.

A storm nearly ripped loose a large branch from a towering pine tree; the brown broken branch stands out against the lush green woods. At any moment it could crash to the ground, but it hangs on. When it stops raining, number two grandson, Shawn, will climb the ladder, and the chain saw will take care of that ugly brown branch.

It's dark this morning; the birds and my neighbors are still asleep. Across the road the university campus is enjoying the calm before the opening of another school year.

The broken branch reminds me of broken people I have met across the endless miles. A storm got to them and they snapped; now they hang, lifeless, cut off from family, church and community.

When I was in New York I met a homeless man in a yellow slicker, pockets bulging with food from a nearby church. I stopped to talk with him and was surprised at his articulate speech.

"Do you have a family, Jim?"

"My parents are dead and the others don't want me now. I was educated at private schools and went into journalism, and then I hit a roadblock. I fell in love with a beautiful girl from Holland, but she decided I wasn't for her."

"Oh, I'm so sorry. She missed an interesting man, if you ask me."

"Do you really think so?"

"Of course I do! She blew it!"

For a moment a smile tugged at the corners of his mouth, but his eyes grew misty. "Thank you, thank you. You know how it is in a storm when a tree crashes across the road and the cars have to take a detour. That's what happened to me. A storm came across my way and I backed off too far."

"Oh, I'm so sorry, Jim, but God is always there, just where you backed off. You can't go too far from Him."

We were quiet. Memories can bless, and they can burn.

Someone called to me and I had to say good-bye. Impulsively I hugged him and kissed his cheek. "That is from your mother."

He stood still and softly added, "Thanks for talking to me."

"Go back to that church," I urged, "and talk to the pastor. You should write about the homeless. And remember, God is right where you backed away. You can begin again."

He walked away, lonely and afraid, a broken branch ready to fall. I think of him often. Maybe, just maybe, he didn't crash, but even if he did, God would pick him up.

Sometimes I feel like a broken branch hanging by a splinter. I know that is not true because I am a branch rooted into the true Vine, Jesus Christ. But after fifty-three years of two branches being one, I find myself a lonely, broken branch. My big lovable Dane went from my arms into the arms of his loving heavenly Father. Within moments one branch was Home, and I was suddenly alone.

With my children's arms around me I heard, "This is the time to give thanks for what we know, not what we see. We know God is sovereign and He never failed you, and He won't fail you now."

What I feel at times is not necessarily true, but the all-alone feeling is there, especially in airports and crowds. I want to be home where nothing has changed, with Harold there holding us all close and telling his funny stories. We all felt safe—no hanging branches.

I must get that branch cut down; it looks so ugly and brown. Doubt and bitterness can turn a green branch brown, and I don't want to hang by a splinter. I long to be a fruitful branch, drawing from the Living Vine.

What we see and feel can dim our eyes with tears, so I speak often about the battle to believe—not what we feel or see, but what we know.

"Lo, I am with you alway" (Matthew 28:20). That we know. The mind battles but the heart cries out in faith, "God is here. I am not alone."

At the last conference I reminded the beautiful young women before me that marriage can be rough and stormy at times, and the early years especially are filled with difficulties and trials, but, "Fight for your marriage," I urged. "Your mate is your precious gift from God, the one you belong to, and the one who belongs to you. No one can ever fill the place of your life's companion."

The widows wiped their eyes, but faces of faith shone through the tears.

The sun is finally coming through the clouds and the green branches stretch toward the heavens. A gentle breeze shakes the drops from the leafy arms of the tree. Only the broken branch hangs by a splinter.

I'll be glad to get that branch down, that reminder of what I could be without Christ—broken, twisted and bruised.

Refreshed from the rain, the hanging baskets looked toward the sun while the brilliant zinnias stretched for a new day. The gardens were alive with color.

Saturday I leave my safe place in the breakfast nook, with the bay window overlooking the flower garden, and I climb the blue skies to Canada.

The broken branch hasn't fallen yet, but now I see some green—hope for broken hearts.

19

Table for One

I was back in "lonesome town" one night during the Christmas season of 1992. The wind whipped the rain against the glass doors of my hotel room in Toronto, Canada. That delightful city, teeming with multicultural people, shouldn't be called lonesome town, except for that night, and by me.

In a dining room filled with couples, I had to ask for a table for one. At home, surrounded by family and friends, I seldom ate alone. This night, though, I sat alone—with Harold across from me in memory.

A plaintive song floated across the room while the rain beat a steady accompaniment against the windows. While I sipped my hot tea, I wondered about other lonely people who sip tea in a silent world of memory. I thought about the brave single mother, rushing home from work to prepare a quick supper for hungry, demanding children. In the silence of memory she saw a happier time when Daddy was home. Then he closed the door and walked away.

At the same time there could be a lonely father somewhere trying to explain why Mommy won't be home.

I could imagine a widow across town rocking in an old chair, with a picture album on her lap and a tear in her eye.

I remembered an elderly man shuffling into the cafeteria to watch the world in motion. He also took a table for one.

There were so many things I wanted to tell Harold, but you can't talk at a table for one. The year before, he had been with me, and I wanted to tell him about the wonderful people I had met this time where I had been a guest earlier that day.

On the talk show we laughed and told Christmas stories, stories of faith and courage, and stories full of humor that bring hope for the future.

I wanted to tell Harold about those people reaching out to the world to feed the hungry, to build camps for children, and to provide shelter for the homeless. But the greatest reach of all was to bring the good news of hope: "God loves you."

Oh, how I wanted to talk about God, who led us through shady green pastures as well as the storms of life. So many things I wanted to tell Harold, but then he already knew. And you can't talk at a table for one.

I had to tell myself that the God who never failed me in my youth won't fail me now when I'm alone and my steps are slower and my eyes grow dim with tears.

The day came to an end and I left the table for one, secure in God's love. When morning came I checked the shuttle bus schedule, then headed for the coffee shop—and another table for one.

I was going home! What a wonderful word, home!

Hot coffee, the aroma of bacon sizzling, and English muffins with marmalade seemed a good way to begin the day.

This time, about my third cup of coffee, an old song came back to me that reminded me of that day when no one will sit at a table for one.

The One who fed the multitudes will call us to sit at His table, a table not for one but for all.

The Light of Home! Grandma can put away her album and open her Bible. "Let not your heart be troubled; I have a place for you."

Grandpa can leave the cafeteria and shuffle back to his lonely room, but when he opens the Bible he will read: "Lo, I am with you; you are not alone." In the silence of memory he can see the faces of his loved ones in the Light of Home.

The single parents, with broken dreams, can find comfort and encouragement within the pages of the Book: "Even if you walk through the shadow of death [death of dreams or of loved ones], don't be afraid. I'll walk with you."

Across the world, tears stain the pages of the Book while God speaks through His words to broken lives and broken hearts.

We can't see or even imagine the glories God has prepared for those who love Him, but we can see through eyes of faith and stand tall as we face another day.

The heroes of everyday living don't often make the headlines except in the news column of heaven, a book of remembrance where even tears are recorded. There is coming a day when tears will be wiped away, losses will be gain, wrongs will be made right, and the stretches and reaches of God's faithful people will see the harvest, where the homeless, the hopeless and the lonely will come marching in, part of the parade of saints.

Rich or poor, famous or unknown, from every tribe and nation—all coming Home because they found the Way, the Truth and the Life, Jesus Christ, the path to the Father's house. No more table for one; the Light of Home sets the table for all.

It was time to leave and I'm sure my thoughts were heard by Harold, even at my table for one.

Then came baggage, shuttle, customs and the boarding call, and I was flying toward home.

It was night when I saw the lights of Wilmington; Ralph and Chris would be there, and we'd have a cup of tea before I unpacked.

P.S. Next time I go to "lonesome town," I'll take Kathryn Elise, my eleven-year-old granddaughter, with me. I can see Katie now, walking with confidence into the coffee shop. "Table for two, nonsmoking. Thank you."

20

The Road Back

"When did you meet Papa?"

As a family we often linger after a meal, and sometimes questions regarding the past come from the children. They are encouraged to express their thoughts. And, believe me, that is not a problem for Sarah and Katie.

To me it is sad that some families don't allow the freedom of expression. Not true in our family! Jud encourages the young people to discuss even their radical views—without getting into an argument. That takes God's grace for me!

But Jud is right. It is wisdom to allow the young to beat their words against the rock of our faith; just so we know in whom we have believed, and having made all the arguments, we still stand on the firm foundation, God's biblical perspective.

"Come on, Grammy, when did you meet Papa? Was it love at first sight?"

"Once upon a time, many years ago, Harold visited my father's church in Chicago and he heard me sing a solo, 'Why Should He Love Me So?' He told everyone I was singing for him. I was sixteen years old.

"No, it wasn't love at first sight, but a deep friendship formed out of our mutual love for the Lord and our desire to know God's will for our lives. This quiet friendship continued through nursing and seminary years. During my training years at Norwegian American Hospital in Chicago, Harold brought candy and apples to my dormitory, probably to win help from my classmates.

"Since I had grown up with an explosive father, Harold's quiet thoughtfulness won me over. One year after graduation we were married. Believe it or not, he was shy and quiet."

"Oh, no! Not Papa."

"Oh, yes, your Papa!"

"Well, you'd never know it. He shook hands with everyone, and no one was a stranger to him."

"On 'romantic' Saturday nights we would attend rescue missions, dish out soup and sandwiches, sing duets, and pray with people. Not too 'cool,' huh?"

Katie chimed in. "I wish I had a tape of your duets."

"I've often thought of that. One of my regrets is that I didn't tape Harold reading the Scriptures. Your Aunt Jan is the only one I know who makes Scripture come alive like Papa Harold did, so full of drama."

"I miss Papa's reading the Christmas story." Eric used to complain because we couldn't open presents until Papa read the Christmas story. Now he misses the reading!

"We don't realize how traditions are missed until they are gone. So I hope you remember to continue those special times when you have your families, just like your parents do, and Aunt Jan and Uncle Jud."

Ralph continued. "I remember when right after supper Jan, Dan, and I would groan, 'Oh, no! Here comes Mother with the Bible and the *Reader's Digest.*'"

"Guess what they missed when they went away to college."

"Chocolate cake!" This from Eric.

"Probably that too! But they also missed the stories."

Someone groaned! Eric?

"Before TV or even radio, your great-grandmother entertained us with long memorized story poems. Whenever a crisis hit our family (a regular occurrence), my Norwegian Mama said, 'Oh, Ja, it will be interesting to see how God works this one out.' Then she would pray and ideas would come.

"In order to enter nurse's training I had to have three hundred dollars, a fortune back then, but Mama cashed an insurance policy that gave me the money. When I went to work at Lutheran Deaconess Hospital after graduation, I paid her back, all three hundred dollars.

"Before Papa and I were married he saved enough money by walking miles to work and school so he could buy a car and pay for our honeymoon to Niagara Falls. That was 1938.

"We lived during the difficult Depression years and Papa's high school education was interrupted so he could help support his family. He went to work at the Bunte Candy Company in Chicago, but he continued his education through correspondence courses. Later he entered Northern Baptist Seminary in Chicago.

"When Mr. Bunte found out that Harold had decided to enter seminary, he tried to get Harold to change his mind by offering him a lucrative position in the company. However, when he understood Harold's determination, he offered his respect and gave Harold a part-time job at full salary.

"Aunt Jan was born in 1940 and I stayed home to care for her. Our food budget was seven dollars a week. Believe me, I learned well from my Norwegian Mama—and we made it!"

"Wow, seven dollars a week! Grammy, Eric spends that at Swensens' on one meal!"

"No wonder Papa liked to take us out to eat. Didn't you ever go to a restaurant?"

"I remember one time. Before Jan was born I just couldn't eat. One night Harold came home from work and classes (sixteen hours, a full load) and suggested we go for a walk. 'Maybe you'll feel better,' he said.

"We passed a Danish restaurant on North Avenue and the menu in the window read 'roast duck.' We stood there for a long time while Harold counted his money. Finally, he said, 'Come on, Margaret. Let's do it!' We ordered the duck dinner and I relished every bite, the first enjoyable meal I'd had in weeks.

"When we would look back over the years, Papa and I would realize we had made some mistakes—financially, some big ones!"

"But Mom, how can you be sure they were mistakes? God still works all things together for His good."

"I know, Ralph, that is the grace of God, and He also judges the heart. David in the Bible made some blunders, but he was a man after God's own heart. In spite of his sin he never lost his love for the one true God. Out of all that tragedy came the Psalms, which comfort and encourage people to this day."

Ralph said, "Man's concept of God can be distorted by our own ideas. I remember the night I led a young man who had been addicted to drugs to the Lord. He actually believed that God would make him marry the ugliest girl in town and ask him to do work he despised.

"I laughed with him about that because I had those same weird ideas before I became a Christian. And look who God gave me—Chris, the most beautiful girl in town. He's blessed us with four children, and I'm doing the work I love, creating furniture in wood."

"By God's Spirit within us," I said, "we enhance the talent He gave us, but when we get too involved in 'ministry,' as defined by others, we don't see the whole picture, only the urgency of the immediate. Now, Harold would see the end from the beginning, but the mistakes loom larger for me when I look back.

"But the Bible warns us not to dwell on the past. Instead, it urges us to run the race and keep looking forward. We always hope that the next generation will profit from the mistakes we made.

"When Harold was working at Bunte and attending classes, I felt like a queen in our tiny bungalow apartment, enjoying the most beautiful baby in the world, our Janice Dawn. But one day Harold came home with the announcement that the pastorate of a small suburban church had been offered to him. He was elated!

"In those early years wise counseling was scarce. It was considered 'spiritual' to launch out by faith, when full-time service meant the mission field or the pastorate. So 'by faith' we left the security of our little world to move into the more 'spiritual' zone of ministry.

"The inadequate salary forced me to work the night shift in nursing while I continued the role of wife, mother, hostess, teacher, church pianist, and pastor's wife.

"After Harold graduated from seminary, he continued his education at Loyola University in Chicago. Because of his evangelistic zeal, he also visited people door to door, on top of his school work. Needless to say, his schedule was quite frantic. I played my part well, but in the lonely watches of the night I wondered how this could be God's will for my life. Bitterness and resentment slipped quietly into the cracks of doubt while the 'dedicated ministry' stayed on course.

"Then a well-meaning Christian urged Harold to give up his Standard Oil stock and insurance. 'It must be a walk of faith,' this man said. In his commitment to walk by faith, Harold allowed wisdom to take a back-road detour.

"Your Papa was an excellent student and several scholarships were offered to him that would have helped him fulfill his dream of a doctor's degree for teaching, or his secret dream, medicine. But in the urgency of the moment, to win the world for Christ, he couldn't see the broader scope of opportunity, and he closed the door.

"God says 'Be still and know,' but we heard, 'Be strong and go'! Down the corridors of time, we learned that all work is 'full-time ministry': the mechanic under a car, a pilot above the clouds, a captain sailing the seas-all of humanity, with a heart for God, making God visible in the marketplace.

"Along the way, Harold often was offered lucrative business opportunities, but once again he was warned against 'pride and riches.' In our day it was considered 'spiritual' to be poor and struggling. How often we keep running with a 'work, for the night is coming' mentality when God's loving hand is reaching out to bless us.

"No one wants to remember the mistakes of the past, but perhaps you precious grandchildren can learn to wait on the Lord, trust God's goodness, and not be driven by the demands of the present. God is our Father and He loves us, but we often see Him as a judge demanding performance rather than as a Father longing for our love and trust."

It was getting late.

Shawn, tall and serious with an intense kind of dedication, wrapped his arms around me. "I don't want to miss God's purpose, Grammy, I don't want to miss it. But I don't think Papa missed anything. He never lost his love for God, and look how we all love him! But I don't want to miss God's purpose for me."

Our children remembered that we never went to Swensens' for hamburgers when they were young. That was a tragedy!

Chris and Ralph, with tears in their eyes, remembered what could have been, but with a deep understanding knew what was—the latter years were greater than the former. God's grace!

The time came for everyone to go home, as it always does. The children were ushered out the door. Eric squealed his way out of the driveway and the house was quiet. The grandfather clock said good night twelve times, but I walked into Harold's library and sat in his leather chair.

The treasured volumes looked down at me, and through the tears I realized that the world had missed a great teacher. He was at home in a classroom or in the business world. But zeal without wisdom had brought us to struggling churches during changing times.

> There is a tide in the affairs of men,
> Which taken at the flood, leads on to fortune;
> Omitted, all the voyage of their life
> Is bound in shallows and in miseries.[1]

On the shelf was the last book Harold read before God took him Home, *The Second Coming,* by C. H. Spurgeon.

I turned out the light and crawled into the empty bed with the teddy bear in the corner. God covered me with His blanket of peace; I was secure in His love.

Harold was Home! Safe! Nothing could hurt him again, and I was thankful that commitment to God and to each other was a fact, not an option. In my childhood I learned to trust the Lord; by God's grace we stayed on course and didn't turn around.

The grandfather clock tried one more time to say good night. One chime told me a new day was on the way, and I fell asleep.

21

The Deep South

"How in the world did you two ever get into the deep South, all the way from Chicago?"

We were asked that question repeatedly, and sometimes even we wondered how it happened.

In the early 1950s, Harold was called to be the pastor of a rural church, deep in the heart of Dixie. Though we would later call this town "Heartbreak Town," we loved the people, the beautiful fairyland setting with flowering magnolia trees, banks of colorful azaleas, and a wonderland of pink and white dogwoods and crepe myrtle trees.

A spacious old farmhouse sat by the side of the road, and that's where we stayed until our small house, which was in the building stage, was completed.

The genuine love of a gentle yet colorful people lives deep in my memory. The elderly were respected, and we watched them rock on their porches while shelling peas or telling stories. Children played while chickens scratched for corn and dogs chased cats.

Church homecomings and family reunions were a way of life where young and old belonged together. No one has really lived until he has experienced a Southern "dinner on the grounds" or an all-day "camp-meeting singing."

When I was introduced to country ham, sweet potato pie and black-eyed peas, I became an instant Southerner. You would have loved it, Eric, tables of Southern cooking, especially Southern fried chicken, biscuits, and corn bread. Your Papa ate three helpings of Miss Lottie's strawberry pudding. I stopped him before his fourth.

Someone asked Miss Lottie, "What do these Yankees eat?"

Miss Lottie answered, "Everything and anything, but mostly my strawberry pudding."

I had warned the children—Jan, Dan and Ralph— to take a bite of everything, and to be polite.

One day Jan overdid it. "This is delicious. Oh, this is very good."

Dan had listened long enough. "Oh, come on, Jan. You know it is not nearly as good as Mother's cooking."

Fortunately our Southern hostess thought it was hilarious, and she kept a special place in her heart for Dan. "A mama's boy if I ever saw one," she insisted.

The country church began to grow and soon was filled with young and old. Within a short time I organized a youth choir of thirty-five members. One lady made robes, and how the youth loved to march in singing, "Everybody ought to know who Jesus is."

A Down's syndrome boy longed to join the choir, and when he received his robe, he marched in with the others—one proud, happy teenager. During the Sunday evening services the young people in the choir often quoted Scripture and gave a personal witness of their faith in Jesus Christ. One evening, our "special boy" began to speak. Slowly, and with difficulty, he said, "Jesus loves me; I love Jesus, and I know it in my heart." There wasn't a dry eye in the crowd.

Harold managed to find a former band leader back in the mountains. Bitter and disillusioned with church, the man had withdrawn from fellowship, but Harold made him feel special and needed. And so our church in the country had a band. Jan played the trumpet and others took lessons.

Since industry from the North was moving into the South, our country church had visitors from the city who enjoyed Harold's fine Bible teaching and the sound of joyful music.

But from the sidelines we heard grumblings. "Change coming. Yes, sir, change coming. Before long we can't wear overalls to church, with city slickers coming in coats and ties. Yes, sir, change coming.

"Now give me that good old hell-fire-and-brimstone preaching any day. I always said an educated preacher is like a drugstore cowboy—no account."

In spite of these misgivings, a spirit of revival filled the air; the church was full on Wednesday night as well as on Sunday.

One Easter Sunday Harold baptized fifteen young people—the future leaders who would make God visible in the marketplace.

One lady took notes all the time but would never let me see them. "I can't spell, but I can tell you this—the only education we get is from our preacher. We're learning about people and history, and he makes the folks in the Bible real folks. I had to quit school to help on the farm, but I'm sure going to school now."

One day I was asked, "Could we have a party on Saturday nights?"

"Of course—but why?"

"Well, the kids at school have parties on weekends, and they make fun of us, so we thought if we had a party at your house, we could tell our friends that we are invited to a party, too."

Party we did! We made candy, had taffy pulls, popped corn, told stories, played games—and sang. How they loved to sing, especially the Youth for Christ choruses that we taught them. "Every day with Jesus is sweeter than the day before" was a favorite.

Papa loved these "kids," and he was always surrounded by them. He opened to them a world of books and music and gave them new challenges toward higher education.

But changes were coming.

"Fool ideas in young'uns heads. What was good enough for my Pappy is good enough for my young 'uns. Heard tell toilets in the church. Well, I never!"

The old-timers rocked on the porch and spat tobacco juice while pulling their overall straps. "Yes, sir, fool women want to run the country. That's what's wrong with the world. Now look at my woman. Says this shack not good enough. Good enough for my Pappy—good enough for us. But she's building a house with cinder blocks. Even made a small room for a bathroom, and wants running water in the house. Never heard of such fool notions.

"That preacher puttin' ideas into their heads; yes, sir, change coming."

One day we were invited to dinner and we forgot to ask about the time, so we decided 12:30 would be about right.

We got to the farmhouse, went in, and there was the head of the family, sitting in his underwear and overalls. Flies buzzed around the screen door as he pulled his overall straps and said, "Dinner in these parts—12 noon. We done et." He spat tobacco juice into the fireplace. "Help yourself."

After a profuse apology we sat down to cold gravy on mashed potatoes. I pinched the children. "Eat and be quiet." Poor Ralph ate—then went outside to throw up. The cold gravy had done its work.

Back on the winding roads of memory I can still smell the sausage and country ham announcing a new day. I can see the mama of one large family pulling sheets of fluffy biscuits out of the old cook stove, and thoughts of her homemade strawberry jam still make my mouth water.

From the porch rocking chairs we heard endless stories, and laughter echoed through the woods.

The love of this big family, who had seen sorrow, sickness, death and disaster, never wavered. In quiet ways their faith remained strong and simple; to us it was an anchor in a time of storm.

Forty years later, the house is gone; the family is gradually having reunions in heaven. "Progress" put a highway where the laughter had been. The rain still cries and the tall pines bend in sorrow.

I recall a happy time when we all gathered in the big yard to enjoy homemade ice cream, and a cold wind suddenly came up. The women put on the coffee pots and we laughed together, with a dish of ice cream in one hand and a cup of hot coffee in the other.

Just as quickly came the cold wind of cultural change and the pot boiled—but it wasn't coffee!

22

The Back Roads to the Past

"Someone tried to shoot Papa."

"Katie, you are making up stories again."

"No, I'm not, Eric. Ask Grammy."

Sarah was furious. "No one would ever want to shoot Papa!" Not her Papa!

"I heard Papa talking about it, so I know someone tried to shoot him. That's not all. Someone saw a big bodyguard sitting beside him and couldn't get at him. I'm not making it up."

Katie, known for her make-believe stories, was determined to get the bits and pieces of this story together, and this was not make-believe. "We'll ask Daddy and Grammy. We weren't even born yet; not even you, Shawn, or Chad, or Heather, but they were there. Aunt Jan was there, too, and someone spat on her. She can tell you about it. And that's not all, either. Someone tried to fire Grammy from the hospital when she was a nurse."

"How come you know so much?"

"Well, Eric, someday I'm going to write a book, so I pay attention to what I hear grown-ups talk about. They didn't know I was listening. Papa's in heaven now so he won't care if I tell."

Shawn turned to Chris, "Mother, you weren't there, but you know about it, don't you?"

"Yes, I do, because your father was there, and he remembers it. Since he was so young no one thought he understood, but he did, and his life was affected by it for many years."

"Why didn't Papa talk about it? He could always tell us."

Sarah and Papa had no secrets—so she thought. Chris said, "Mother, I think you need to tell the story. Heather and Chad need to know the truth."

It was evening in North Carolina, a time when squirrels stopped their play, and the mockingbirds called out, "Good night." The grandchildren needed to know, but it was difficult to begin.

It happened almost forty years ago, and that's a long time to remember. Places and names are not important, but events and causes reflect a difficult era when cultural change was taking place.

I started with a story about *my* papa. "I remember when your great-grandfather Tweten was caught in a cultural conflict. When the immigrants from Norway came to this country, they worked hard to learn a new language. Some who were artists, musicians and writers took jobs in lumber camps, on farms and with domestic services. No one complained—they were thankful for the opportunity to live in America and dream big dreams, especially for their children.

"When the children grew up, they desired to be truly American, so they resisted the old ways. They wanted an American church. Papa Tweten compromised and had Norwegian church Sunday morning and English services in the evening. Later that was changed to English for all the services except for a Norwegian Bible study.

"Looking back I can understand how the immigrants felt. All week they worked in an English-speaking world, and they had to struggle to keep pace with change. When Sunday came they wanted to be in a familiar world with Old Norwegian hymns, and sermons in their familiar tongue. They were home again, if just for a little while!

"The young people moved into higher education, and in some cases they were ashamed of their thick Norwegian accent. Yet they were deeply respectful, and with thankful hearts they blessed their devoted parents.

"From a small congregation we counted about forty young people who were moving into the fields of religion, medicine, business and the arts. These made up the first generation of Norwegian Americans in my father's church. After many years of faithful service, your great-grandfather was voted out of the church in favor of an American pastor.

"Dazed and confused, he wandered from church to church, just a visitor, lost in the crowd. Mama and her children stayed in their regular pew to worship God. Steadfast and immovable in the work of the Lord, Mama prayed and believed that God does work all things together for His good.

"Later, my Papa was called to a church in Brooklyn, New York, where he remained until he retired at eighty-three years of age.

"'God and Mama can do anything!' That's what my father always said.

"So you see, sometimes a person finds himself in the cross fire of change, and he gets wounded. We are all afraid of change, and sometimes fear, not hate, motivates people toward unkind deeds. What I learned during that difficult time was that God is sovereign, and His purpose in our lives is not subject to the winds of change. Just as the Alps aren't swayed by the storms, so we are kept steady by the power of God.

"Your great-grandfather had faults, like his temper, but he never held bitterness or unforgiveness in his heart. He believed God and His Word and he knew God's promises would not fail."

"Wow, I wish we could have known him, Grammy."

"Aunt Jan knew him and loved him. He called her 'Princess.'"

"That's what my Papa called me, his princess." For some reason Sarah knew he had tucked her into a "special princess" corner of his heart.

"Well, Papa called me Queen Kathryn."

"I remember when Heather was born that Grandpa Tweten thought his first great-grandchild was the most beautiful girl in the world. Wouldn't he be proud of her now?"

"I heard that Grandpa Tweten called Uncle Jud a prince. He said, 'Ja, ja, I see the princess has found a prince.'"

"How come Katie knows everything?"

"I listen, Eric."

"Papa and I understood each other," Shawn remembered. "He never said much about what happened when he was a little boy, but he used to say, 'Shawn, you must read the Word of God, and allow God to guide you. Pride can be your greatest enemy. You must keep a humble heart and be quick to ask forgiveness.'"

"I remember a time when Eric and Shawn were very young and Shawn left Papa's tools in the rain."

"Whew, Papa was mad at you, Shawn!" Eric remembered it, too.

"Papa got upset with you, too, Eric. We were all supposed to go to the beach after the rain, but Papa said, 'No beach!'"

Eric added, "Shawn was crying out in the carport, and I told him to tell Papa he was sorry. Shawn kept saying, 'He'll never forgive me, and he won't take us to the beach.'

"I asked him, 'How will you know, if you don't tell him you are sorry?'

"But Shawn was so sure. He cried, 'No, he'll never forgive me.'

"I said, 'Shawn, I'll go tell him for you. You are sorry, aren't you?'

"And he answered, 'Of course I'm sorry, but it's no use. He'll never forgive me.'

"I started toward the study, but then, Grammy, you said, 'You can't ask forgiveness for Shawn. He has to go himself.' Remember?"

"Yes, Eric, I certainly do. You said, 'Come on, Shawn, go ask forgiveness.' You wanted to go to the beach.

"And finally, slowly, sad-faced, Shawn edged his way to Papa's lap. 'I'm sorry, Papa.' Eric and I waited on the porch and we heard Shawn and Papa laughing and then Papa hollered, 'To the beach, everyone!'

"Eric just shook his head, and said, 'Big deal.'

"Shawn and I walked along the beach watching the waves tumble in, and I asked him, 'Shawn, did you realize that Eric tried to go to bat for you?'

"'Yes,' Shawn answered.

"I asked him if he would have done that for Eric, and he answered no.

"'That's the difference between you two boys, and maybe you have something to learn about humility.'

"Several years later, Shawn did go to bat for Eric when he spoke to the basketball coach about Eric's ability and urged the coach to use Eric. That evened the score, even if it took time."

"Grammy," interrupted Sarah, "you are beating around the bush and not getting to the story about who wanted to shoot Papa."

Ralph spoke up. "I can tell Mother doesn't want to remember that, Sarah, but sometimes we have to remember the past so we can deal with the future. It took years before I understood how I was influenced by the past."

"You're right, Ralph. I guess I'd like to close that door, but the children can learn from the past and take courage for the future.

"Our times are in God's hands and He will wind the clock."

23

Heartbreak Town

The story began to come out.

Harold and I traveled the country roads together. We visited shut-ins, sat in kitchens, ate ham biscuit and listened to stories of a long-ago time.

It was here we met the most creative people. One woman with limited education had taught herself to paint. The baptistery scene in the church was the work of her creative heart.

The county voted her Woman of the Year for her creative gifts in cooking, canning, sewing and intricate needlework.

To add to her list of accomplishments, she also was voted the best dressed woman—her *Vogue*-looking outfit was made from feed sacks.

Harold seemed to be motivated twenty-four hours a day, seven days a week—remodeling and painting the church, visiting people scattered in a rural community, spending time with alcoholics and troubled people. His greatest joy was to encourage young people to dream dreams.

If these young people could create beauty out of their hearts of love, there was no limit to what they could do—at home or elsewhere in the world.

He never stopped. He worked tirelessly to build a strong rural church that would send young people into the marketplace to reveal God's love.

When Harold was on one of his treks through the surrounding hill country, he came upon a group of trees that seemed to have shotguns for arms.

Scraggly children hid in the bushes.

Harold called out, "I'm looking for Uncle Zeb."

"Ain't no one here; and you—who you be? 'A revenuer'?"

"No, I'm a preacher, not a revenue officer. How about coming to church sometime?"

The guns were put away; the moonshiners gave clear passage, and Harold made his exit. Later someone said, "Why, preacher, you could have been shot. Those hill folks don't take kindly to strangers. They'd shoot a man over a dog."

The church continued to grow, but when we returned from a visit with Harold's parents, it appeared the town had begun to take on a heartbreaking aspect. One of the deacons said, "Preacher, all hell broke loose while you were gone. A rumor was started that you were a Communist and a nigger lover. Folks are saying you should be tending to preaching and not to all that social gospel of bringing food and clothes to the no-good white trash in the hills.

"Some folks said that the Salvation Army and Youth for Christ were Communist fronts. And some

folks go so far as to say Billy Graham is no account—
him a Baptist and letting all them other folks, no telling
what they are, sit on the platform.

"We know that's not true, but when a lie gets
rolling in these hills, no telling if it's gonna collect a
mob. I remember how you stood up for Billy Graham
at the preachers' meeting when they were criticizing
him. You said, 'Until we do what Billy is doing to win
the lost, we have nothing to do but pray and support
him.'

"The preachers have turned against you. I heard
about it, so I'm warnin' you, some angry people
around."

"Well, I guess people are afraid of change," Harold
responded, "but all I want is to see a thriving church
reaching into all the area, including the town."

We couldn't believe those things were true, and we
continued the work.

Harold found a family of seven sick in a shack and
took them to the emergency room. Hepatitis! The dedicated doctor who worked the emergency room must
have bemoaned Harold's coming.

Another time Harold found a mother and her children huddled under threadbare quilts in a frigid shack.
Pneumonia! Harold went to a town merchant and got a
stove. When he brought it to the husband he said,
"Now, put this stove up so it will be warm for your
family. Don't forget to chop enough wood. I have to
leave, but I'll be back in the morning."

When Harold returned the next morning he found
the stove right where he had left it.

"Well, preacher, just didn't get around to it."

Harold was furious, so he put the stove together himself and started a fire. "Now, you chop wood or I'll get the authorities out here!"

"Ain't no preacher business, you comin' out here to tell me what to do."

One day Harold marched seven children into a shoe store, and all seven came out with new shoes. The merchants admired him! "That preacher's doing more than all the churches put together."

Then they heard the rumors and warned Harold to leave. "This community needs you, preacher, but you don't need them. Get your family out. Rumors have a way of building up to real trouble around here."

"It's all so ridiculous! I hate communism with a passion—a godless, controlling government that stifles all creativity and motivation. Jesus said, 'If I be lifted up . . . I will draw all men unto me'—so if I continue to preach the truth, men's hearts will turn to God."

One day during this uproar, Jan asked, "Mother, I was walking down the street and a woman spat on me—someone I knew; why would she do that?"

"See, Eric? I didn't make it up," Katie broke in. "Someone did spit on Aunt Jan. She told me. But she didn't spit back; she just kept walking. I'm not sure I could do that."

"Well, what would you do, spit back? Pretty soon everyone would run out of spit. Ha! She did the right thing—keep on walking and scrub the spit off."

"Well, Grammy, what else happened?"

Papa and I often followed the school bus and waved to our young people on the bus. Then when they got off the bus, we would spend a few minutes chatting with them.

One day we followed the bus and no one waved back. When they got off the bus they turned their backs to us. We sat in the car and cried! This was our youth group! What had happened?

One brave girl whispered to Jan, "It's not us—our Pappy made us. Tell the preacher not to come near our house. Pappy has a gun."

"Tell about the night our Papa was on the road," Katie interrupted again.

"Harold was used to taking a dirt road shortcut. Later someone asked, 'Who is that preacher's bodyguard? I was waiting beside the road to take a shot at him—but I couldn't get to him. A big bodyguard was sitting next to him.'"

Katie interrupted, "There was no bodyguard! Papa said it had to be an angel. I wish I could see an angel, but Papa didn't even see him. I guess there are lots of things we don't understand. Do you believe in angels, Grammy?"

"Yes, I do, Katie, because once when I got off a streetcar in Chicago, many years ago, I was standing on the safety platform. A large truck came zooming toward the safety zone. Someone grabbed me and pulled me to the curb. A man came running over. 'Wow! I never saw anything like it. You jumped to the curb like you were flying'.

"'Someone pulled me,' I answered.

"'Oh, no, lady, no one was near you.'

"I just said, 'Thank You, Lord,' and I always thought it had to be an angel. There are some things we can't understand."

Well, getting back to the story.

The phone started to ring around the clock and disguised voices called us vulgar names and threatened to get me fired from the hospital. In fact, a delegation went to the hospital board. I heard about it later.

Our Doberman kept constant watch around our home, alert for impending danger. I'm sure this beautiful dog protected us from harm more times than we will ever know. Later, when she was poisoned, we grieved her loss.

Now it was Ralph's turn. "I was so young and that was my special dog. She stood watch over me when I was two and had a broken leg. Our Vickie would growl when anyone touched my cast to sign it.

"One day I saw a man being mean to my dog, and hate began to build up inside of me. Everyone thought I was too young to know what was going on, but I wasn't.

"Now, forty years later, I see it for what it really was—spiritual warfare. It was not men, but unseen powers and principalities working through men's fears and hate to destroy God's work. For years ignorance and prejudice ruled me, but now the light of God's truth and understanding comes filtering through the darkness. Darkness hates light."

"You are so right, Ralph, but at that time we did not understand spiritual warfare like we do today, and we were so convinced that truth and right would win.

"The war is ultimately already won. We can lose battles along the way, though, because we do not understand the great warfare. It still rages against God and His purpose for His church."

We learned many years later that our weapons of logic and reason were not enough. The Scriptures we had memorized took on new meaning in the battle of experience. We must put on the whole armor of God so we can stand against the wiles of the devil (see Ephesians 6). We don't wrestle against people but against rulers of darkness.

"I think of all you precious grandchildren—Heather, Chad, Shawn, Eric, Sarah, and Kathryn, and your cousins and friends. Your conflict will not be the same as the conflict of the fifties, or even the eighties. But I do see a great conflict looming like a cloud on the horizon; it will be a war of values.

"What has been an established Judeo-Christian heritage for two hundred years suddenly is attacked, and the war wages to brainwash the American mind into 'political correctness' (PC). Will you young people dare to voice what may not be considered 'PC' by a few?

"Where will the independent voices be that sounded the trumpet against the injustice of slavery? To some it would not have been 'politically correct' to go against that tide.

"During World War II, the concentration camps overflowed with those who dared to condemn injustice. In the nineties, will the soul of America bend into another kind of slavery—the fear of speaking the truth about the values that can preserve a society?

"I sometimes fear that you children will find yourselves in the prison of conformity unless you really know who you are in Christ Jesus, and have a deep understanding of God's purpose in each life in a church, in society and in the world."

"But Grammy, the world is changing so fast, and we have to be educated to think for ourselves and use logic and understanding."

"That's true, Shawn, but logic and knowledge must be filtered through the wisdom of God's Word. God's laws don't change. The Ten Commandments apply to this time also. We need the mind of Christ to understand the changing times.

"Papa and I had little understanding of the changing times of the fifties. God knew our hearts and our love for Him and the people, but that wasn't enough. We needed more. We needed to know how the power of the Holy Spirit moves in people's hearts. Logic can change minds, but only God's Spirit can change hearts.

"It took many years before we realized the truth of Zechariah 4:6: 'Not by might, nor by power, but by my spirit, saith the LORD.' We didn't know it then, but God's protective love covered us and kept us safe.

"You may not realize how the forces of darkness battle to destroy our Christian values, but now is the time to dig your heels in and stand on the sure foundation, Jesus Christ.

"Oswald Chambers says,

> The Holy Spirit supplies the atonement to us in the unconscious realm as well as in the realm of which we are conscious.... To walk in the Light means that everything that is of the darkness drives me closer into the centre of the light.[1]

"I want to remind you precious children that the battle is lost or won in the secret places of the will before God.

"There may come a time when you have to make a sudden choice, and the choices we make will affect everyone around us. If we settled our relationship with God in our youth and purposed to do His will, then the choices we make later will be determined in light of His Word. Unless we walk in the light of God's Word we can be slaves to a point of view that is alien to Christ.

"The day came, in what we had begun to think of as 'Heartbreak Town,' when your Papa had to make a choice."

24

The "Storm"

It was Wednesday night and we hurriedly ate supper to get to church on time for our weekly Bible study and prayer.

As we wound our way through town toward the country road that led to our country church, we noticed heavy traffic and police cars. Drawing closer to the church, we saw a mob outside, with police cars surrounding the church yard. When we pulled into the side road we were met by a giant of a man, a former security guard, who whispered, "Get inside! I'll park the car. There's a rockin' planned."

"A rockin'? What is that?" Katie wanted to know. We found out.

"Remember when a mob stoned Stephen? Well, that's a rockin'." This came from Ralph. "No one thought I heard things, but I guess I was like Katie. I didn't miss much that older people said. There were moonshiners who had come down from the hills, prisoners who had been released from jail, prostitutes, and others who hadn't darkened the doors of the church for decades—all had shown up for that midweek service.

"A menacing crowd stood facing the road—the rockin' crowd—ready to throw rocks at us and our car. Suddenly we were all gripped with fear, all but Dad. His face was white, but it was more from anger than fear.

"Mama kept whispering, 'God will take care of us,' but we weren't too sure!

"Jan, Dan and I sat on the front pew, on the side where Mama played the piano. Jan had her arms around us. I was four, Dan was nine, Jan was thirteen. We were too frightened to cry, and we just sat huddled together. Mama was shaking, but she went to the piano.

"I remember how Daddy looked, like a giant, so tall and straight, when he announced the opening hymn. Mama played, and we sang 'Trust and Obey'—loud! We were so scared.

"A women jumped up on a pew and screamed, 'I move we have the conference!'

"Daddy told her to sit down and be quiet. 'This is not conference night, but the regular midweek service.'

"I looked around and saw people sitting in the open windows, standing everywhere, inside and outside. Police cars were all over the place. Later, I learned some of the people even had guns.

"A man ran down the aisle threatening to kill Daddy, but the big security guard sat him down."

"I can't believe you remember so much, Ralph. I thought you were too young. I can still see Jan with her protective arms around you boys. I was shaking at the piano, but Harold was quiet and calm. He had made his choice to stand true to the purpose God had called him to.

"I will never forget how Harold stood up. 'This is our regular midweek service, and there will be order while we turn to Hebrews 12:27: "Removing of those things that are shaken, as of things that are made, that those things which cannot be shaken may remain." The topic tonight is "The Unshakable in a Changing World."'"

I stopped and looked at the young faces around me.

"I can't believe I'm holding his Bible, with tiny notes only he could read and the pages all worn and torn. Harold also had a small pocket Bible that he kept with him, besides shelves of study Bibles in many translations. He always came back to the King James Version because he had memorized entire books in that translation. It was a part of him.

"I will see to it that the Bibles are given to you grandchildren. I'll keep the old one, worn with use and tears.

"So this is where I'll turn in his Bible—Hebrews 1:8: 'Thy throne, O God, is for ever and ever: a sceptre of righteousness is the sceptre of thy kingdom.'"

I resumed my story.

A quiet came over the crowd that night, and all of a sudden I stopped shaking. This was the unshakable Word of God.

Harold's voice continued:

1. The throne of God is unshakable in a changing world.
2. Psalm 119—The Word of God is unshakable in a changing world. The Word is forever settled in heaven. The Word is true from the beginning; it endureth forever.
3. The church of God—Matthew 16:18: "Upon this rock [Thou art the Christ, the Son of the living God] I will build My church; and the gates of hell shall not prevail against it." The church of God is unshakable in a changing world.
4. The child of God—John 3:16 . . .

Harold closed with the story of a great preacher who had been told he had a short time to live. While this preacher watched the splendor of the sunset over his beloved mountains he said, "When the sun has set for the last time, and the mountains melt away, I, the child of God, shall live on."

Harold pronounced the benediction and with quiet dignity left the platform, leaving a dazed mob.

I remember telling the children later, "You will always remember this night—your father's finest hour."

Our big friend grabbed the children and hurried us to the car, and he urged us, "Leave town. Go to Florida for a week and perhaps this mob will quiet down."

We took a back road home, and then we packed and left town, quiet and confused.

Jan cried, "Daddy, fight them in court. Get a lawyer."

Dan answered quietly, "Jan, someday we'll all stand before the Lord, and if they talked about us, so what? But the ones who did the talking—oh, brother!"

Ralph said nothing. We thought he was too young. How wrong we were!

When we returned, the church was locked and the wonderful people whom we loved wept with us. The young people especially cried, "Now who will love us?"

"Mother, you forgot something!" Ralph spoke up. "When the security guard pushed us into the car, a man ran up to the window beside Dad and yelled some terrible things. I reached from the back seat and punched him in the nose. 'You don't talk to my Daddy like that.'

"Then Dad did something that I misunderstood. He put me down in the back seat and said, 'That's not the way we do things.'

"Many years later I realized it was that incident that triggered such a big rebellion in me. A smoldering hate began in me and I lumped all Christians together, including my own Dad—they were all wimps!

"Dad didn't even stand up for me. To me he was defending the wrong people. A deep resentment grew out of that misunderstanding. From that day, when I was four years old, until I was born again at twenty-one, I was in one fight after another. My fists were the way for me to conquer.

"Do you remember, Shawn, when you mistook something I said and went to bed crying? Then I climbed up in the bunk bed and held you in my arms and said, 'Now, you tell me what I said.' When you told me, it was not what I had said at all. You had heard the wrong voice.

"In that instant I began to weep. God's Spirit showed me how I had heard the wrong voice so many years ago. Then I was angry—angry at the devil for cheating me out of years that could have been filled with love and peace instead of fear and fists.

"Now, Shawn and Eric, don't you listen to the wrong messages and get confused. You must hear God's still, small voice. I guess that's one reason to return to the past, so we can learn from it and deal with the future better."

Oswald Chambers said, "Leave the irreparable past in His hands, and step out into the irresistible future with Him."[1]

Forty years ago the future looked dark. The storm in Heartbreak Town had ravaged our hearts and the debris gathered dust. Unforgiveness made a crack in the door, and bitterness slithered in.

25

The Wilderness Journey

"Grammy, tell us how you came to North Carolina."
Katie made sure we kept the story going.

"While we were in Florida Harold was offered a
position in a school, but during that period of frustra-
tion and confusion it was difficult to make a wise decision.

"Looking back, I see it probably would have been a
good move, but it is always easier to see what might
have been when you look back.

"Harold made another choice. 'I'm not going back
into the pastorate,' he declared. Instead, he chose to
form his own company, being a consultant in church
building programs and financing church buildings
through bonds.

"We wept like frightened children when Harold got
in the car to venture into unknown territory. He chose
to locate in Greensboro, the center of North Carolina."

Ralph shook his head. "It took me years to realize
how frightening it must have been for him to go 'cold'

into a new field. I only know how fear gripped me when I moved from Greensboro to Wilmington to begin my own business."

"Dad didn't say much; he just acted confident. But years later he told me how fear had dogged his journey. Only the Word of God kept him going. For me, I had to keep saying that God didn't give me the spirit of fear, but of love, of power, and of a sound mind.

"Dad told me something else, too. 'I learned to go to the top official in business dealings,' he said, 'and not to settle for an assistant. When I came cold to Greensboro, High Point, and Winston-Salem, I met with the presidents of the largest banks and introduced church-bond financing. I was at home with legal experts in Raleigh and bankers across the state. God gave me "favor with men" and a new door opened in North Carolina.'"

Grammy continued the tale. "Lexington Avenue Baptist Church in High Point was the first church built by bonds. Harold and the pastor remained friends for years. There is something special about a person's first success story.

"We didn't know too much about what Harold did because the churches were scattered throughout the state. But when I went through Harold's papers after he died, I found letters from pastors all over the state. One of them said: 'Not only did we have fund-raising success but there also was a spirit of revival and people came to the altar. Not only was there a giving of money but also a giving of self to serve the Lord.'

"I saw through those letters how the pastors of both black and white churches respected Harold and called him 'the pastor's friend.' I remember how he bought evangelical books for the pastors' libraries and enjoyed visiting in the homes of the black pastors where he ate 'chitlins' and swapped stories. One pastor was having a difficult time in his marriage, so Harold gave him money to take his wife on a vacation.

"It was difficult for me to adjust my thinking from the pastorate, of which I had been a part since child-hood, to financing buildings, when all my life I had been involved in building people. But God, through His Holy Spirit, opened my eyes and made me realize that all of us are in 'full-time service,' making God visible in the marketplace."

"Did Papa ever go back to Heartbreak Town, Grammy?"

"He said, 'I'll never go back' but he did! But that's another story.

"Harold never forgot one special incident from Heartbreak Town. You see, Katie, God uses many different people to show forth His love. After your Papa drove out of town with us all huddled together, he stopped at a rundown gas station.

"An elderly man, stooped from the burden of bygone years, was unshaven and in oil-splattered overalls. He shook his head. 'Preacher, they done you wrong. Yes, sir, preacher, they done you wrong. I don't cotton to church-goin', but I know what goes on. Yes, sir, I know what goes on. What you done was good—but they done you wrong'.

"Harold said, 'His weather-beaten face showed such compassion that I wanted to cry. When I reached into my pocket to pay for the gas, he shook his head, reached into his greasy overalls pocket, and pulled out a one-hundred-dollar bill.'

" 'Preacher, wherever you're goin', God bless you, and yes, sir, they done you wrong.' "

"Harold said later, 'That man never knew how much I needed that hundred-dollar bill, but God knew.' "

"When did you go to North Carolina?"

"Very soon after that, Katie. Your Papa found us a house. After he painted it he came for us.

"We enrolled Janice in a Christian academy for two years; then she went to Wheaton to college. That's where she met Uncle Jud. I worked at Cone Hospital and Harold traveled all over the state."

My world had changed, and I knew it would not be easy to be "in charge" while Harold traveled and lived in motels.

One day Dan and Ralph found me crying. "What's wrong, Mom?"

"I miss Janice," I whispered. "She always set the table and made a fancy centerpiece."

The next day I came home from the store and Dan and Ralph had set the table with my best china and silverware. In the center sat a bowl of weeds. "See, you have us."

"Of course I have you—and what a beautiful table!"

In the meantime, the suppressed pain from Heartbreak Town began surfacing in each of us.

A kindergarten teacher confided to Harold that Ralph drew only animals. "He doesn't like people," she said. And we had thought he was too young to understand.

Jan was popular at school but began keeping her friends at a distance. Trust wouldn't come easily—but then she met Jud and trust returned.

Dan was quiet, ever the obedient son—maybe too good?

Ralph used his fists.

I felt a gnawing apprehension that all was not well in our family, which impelled me to work harder to keep order in the home, supply finances for school, and keep acquaintances at a distance. After all, I had my sisters and my parents. They didn't know the details, but they knew how to pray, and I counted on that.

In our own way, each of us had determined never to be vulnerable again.

Harold drove the endless miles, removed from family affairs, convinced that "Margaret can handle it." I used to think maybe I should have given in to my heart's desire and demanded help.

Our wilderness journey had begun, but we didn't know it.

"I remember the time Dad took us to the dedication of a country church way up in the mountains."

"That's right, Jan."

Jan was home from school and we took coffee and cinnamon rolls in the car, since we had to leave about 5 A.M. We wore old clothes and brought our Sunday clothes along.

"Guess we had better stop and change clothes," Dad said. He didn't have to change—he was always dressed up.

We stopped at a deserted gas station and I was pulling on a girdle (those were the days of tight girdles) when I saw someone move in the gas station.

Two bearded faces, grinning from ear to ear, were watching my battle with the girdle. You can be sure I beat a hasty retreat!

We arrived at the beautiful new church surrounded by tall pines, with mountains in the background. Trucks and cars filled the parking lot.

We walked in together and sat down. The service began.

"Oh, I see Brother Jensen and his family are here. Please stand up so we can greet you. (Applause!) Now, Brother Jensen, we want you up on this platform."

With tears in his eyes the preacher began. "I never thought we'd see the day when we would have such a beautiful church. Brother Jensen came along and showed some simple plans for a building, then said we could do it. He had such faith, and praise God, we did it!"

The church applauded again and the preacher hugged Harold. We watched in awe. We really didn't know much about his work or how his faith inspired others.

The choir leader got excited and announced, "Now we are going to dedicate the choir numbers to the Jensens."

They sang "I'll Fly Away" and "Amazing Grace" and my favorite, "I'm Standing on the Solid Rock." I think the choir leader saw my face and said, "We'll just do that one more time." And they did!

The singing continued, and then came the preaching. The service was followed by dinner on the grounds.

On the way home Harold recounted some humorous stories. "That preacher and I went to see an old tobacco farmer about buying a church bond. He lived in an old run down shack, and we thought he'd perhaps buy a hundred-dollar bond for a grandchild.

"He listened, chewed his tobacco, and then said, 'Ma, git the pot from under the bed.' Ma came out carrying a foul-smelling pot and he said, 'Not that one, Ma, the other one.'

"The foul-smelling pot was put back under the bed, and Ma returned carrying the other pot. When she passed it to Pa, I saw it was full of money. Pa counted ten thousand dollars in cash and bought ten one-thousand dollar bonds.

"Why don't you put that money in the bank?" I asked.

"'Nope, preacher; don't trust no banks.' And Ma put that pot back under the bed."

On our way home we looked for a gas station so we could use the restrooms. We were desperate but we still couldn't find a station. The road was dark, and there were no other cars, so Harold hollered, 'Sorry, no restrooms; everyone find a tree.' We did!

About that time a stream of cars came around the bend. Their headlights formed instant spotlights and horns honked. We had been caught in the act.

Later we found out an accident had caused those cars to detour down our "deserted road."

No one ever forgot the dedication service of that country church.

One day the president of a bank said, "Margaret, you should be so proud of Harold. He brought millions of dollars into the banks of North Carolina and has earned respect from the entire banking community for his integrity. Because of his wise counsel, no church has ever defaulted."

It was then I realized how many churches had been built in North Carolina because of Harold.

Harold enjoyed the freedom of his work, but I felt imprisoned by responsibilities. I was in my own wilderness.

26

Troubled Waters

"Tell about the time someone wanted you fired, Grammy." Katie was determined to hear the whole story.

"Well, Katie, that too happened in Heartbreak Town."

There had been a serious automobile accident and I was helping in the emergency room at the hospital. We quickly determined the most desperate cases that needed immediate attention.

A black woman, dazed and in pain, sat in a corner. I called over to the doctor, "This lady needs attention." Within moments a doctor checked her and admitted her to the hospital.

But a passing visitor heard me say "this lady" and reported me for calling a black woman a lady. "I want her fired!"

The administrator stood up in righteous indignation and replied, "Never! She'll be the last to leave." Tensions were building.

Forty years ago the hospital overlooked a fast-growing city. The Basement, or B section, was reserved for black patients, but the facilities and care were the same throughout the hospital.

A respected black doctor had been educated by a white doctor's family. When invited to eat lunch with the other doctors, he declined and chose to eat with the black janitors. Old ways resist change.

Harold and I had been educated in Chicago with various races and ethnic groups and had little understanding of Southern culture. In hindsight I see that we had bolted in where angels feared to tread.

As assistant director of nurses I often checked the different wards, and my favorite place was the B section. There I heard singing, laughter, tears, stories— and prayers.

One morning I asked Miss Lizzie, a diabetic patient, for a urine specimen.

"Oh, I forgot and just 'weed.'"

"Oh, come on now, just a few drops—try again."

When she produced enough for a specimen, I cheered. "Hurrah for Miss Lizzie. We did it!"

The ward burst into laughter, and when I turned to leave I heard Miss Lizzie. "Lord have mercy! Did you see how excited that nurse got over a little wee?" She chuckled delightedly. "I do believe she's selling it!"

On one of my rounds in the men's ward, Uncle Joe, a hundred years old more or less and in a coma, was dying. His soiled linens demanded attention.

I reached for a basin of water, pulled the curtain, and bathed Uncle Joe like a baby. His white hair framed his black face. Powdered, and in fresh linen,

Uncle Joe looked like a peaceful child. I held his hand and quoted the Twenty-Third Psalm.

When I emerged with the basin and linens, I saw three black men in the other beds, eyes filled with tears.

"Thank you, nurse. Uncle Joe taught us how to read from the Bible. His last wish was, 'I don't want to meet my Maker dirty.'"

Within an hour, Uncle Joe met his Maker—clean.

Another time when I passed the B section, I saw a white woman sitting by the bedside of her old black cook. She was weeping as she gently caressed the wrinkled black face. Her cook was dying.

When I came near she said, "You can't laugh, cry, and raise children together, and not grieve for your best friend." She sat there for hours.

The doctor came and stroked the black face tenderly. "She took care of me since I was a baby, and now I have taken care of her."

The cook died peacefully surrounded by love that knew no barriers.

I have often wondered why these stories of tender love never make the news, these many stories that could smooth troubled waters.

Times were changing. Angry marchers with long-suppressed hostilities were demonstrating with a frenzy. When blacks were railing against the injustices of the whites, I wondered if three black men somewhere would be less angry when they remembered Uncle Joe and his white nurse.

Change comes when hearts are integrated by love—not by laws alone. Hearts segregated by hate can never change; only God's love can melt the barriers and bring lasting understanding.

On one occasion Miss Bessie, one of the black hospital maids, was overcome with grief. Her house had burned and with it the presents under the Christmas tree. The hospital staff rallied and found Miss Bessie a place to live and gathered furniture and household furnishings for her. The chairman of the board had a clothing factory, and within a short time there was clothing for the children and presents under a new tree.

Ample Miss Bessie could never keep her uniform buttoned. Her bosom seemed to pop the buttons, so she used large pins to hold things together. One day the chairman came out of a board meeting and Miss Bessie ran over to him and threw her arms around him, thanking him loud and clear for his generosity.

A quiet, reserved man, he turned—somewhat embarrassed—to see the board members enjoying the scene.

"Good for public relations," someone chuckled.

That gave me an idea! I called the chairman. "How about clothing for all the children of all the black staff? Good for public relations," I chuckled.

So it came to pass that a truckload of clothing came to the hospital. A room was set aside where coats and jackets of all sizes, even matching outfits for a new set of twins, were wrapped and tagged with children's names.

I don't think I ever saw such joy permeate the hospital staff as when those gifts were given for the children. The chairman of the board expressed it for all of us. "Thank you for the happiest Christmas."

By the way, that never made the news. Only hate and strife came out in bold headlines.

Much later, when it was time for me to say good-bye to my hospital friends, I went to the B section. There I found the black staff in a corner weeping.

"What happened? Did someone die?"

"We heard you were leaving!"

They were crying for me! Then I cried.

I loved them, and I still hold their memory in my heart. I can hear their songs while they worked, their stories and laughter at lunch time. I shared their tears and knew of their dreams for their children. When opportunities come later for those children, I only hope that their parents with their mops and brooms aren't forgotten.

It was true when angry whites called me a "nigger lover."

But one day came when I almost lost my song.

27

The Traveling Man

Days, months, years seem to roll into one when urgency-of-the-moment living turns the calendar pages into years. There was no stopping place.

I was on a train and never could get off at my station. There was no one to talk to. The children demanded attention, the bills mounted. The days became a blur of white uniforms, household chores all hours of the night, then collapse into bed with the alarm clock ready to sound my 5:30 A.M. wake-up call. One night my sewing machine purred until 2 A.M. as I finished a banquet dress for Janice at Wheaton.

Birthday parties, school functions, and church became routine. It was a case of survival, one foot in front of the other. Years later I remembered that even survival is victory.

Harold stayed on the road. Oh, how I wished I could hit the open road—but my feet were in the quagmire of duty.

In desperation I cried out, "Harold, you are going to lose Ralph. He cries for you to take him to a game—or do something with him. The day will come when you will cry for him and he will be gone."

That day came. "Harold, we need to talk!" I urged. "I don't have time—I'm due at a meeting."

His car backed out of the driveway and I screamed, "Come back!"

He didn't hear me; no one heard me—it was a silent scream.

"Mother, what's wrong with Daddy? He won't take time to talk about my wedding plans."

"Jan, he won't talk to me, either. He is locked in a prison of his own."

"Let's face it, Mom, he doesn't care about us anymore."

"That's how it seems, Ralph, but it is not true. I believe he is holding unforgiveness in his heart, and bitterness is silently destroying him."

He wouldn't listen so I wrote letters—no response.

He was there for weddings and graduations, and he wept when Dan went to Vietnam, but still he remained in his captive world. He was there—but not there.

When Ralph went to college Harold gave him—over my objection—a car to make up for time not given. It didn't work. It never does. Ralph rebelled by being a part of the sixties hippie movement.

Harold kept traveling, a desperate man looking for peace, but subtle bitterness kept closing the door.

To find our peace, we all have to go back to the fork in the road where relationships were broken. We all have to return to the "hurting place," to our own

Heartbreak Town where only unconditional love and forgiveness can open the door to peace and restoration.

Jan was happily married to Judson Carlberg.

Dan was in Vietnam.

Ralph was in the "far country."

Harold stayed on the road.

In the lonely night watches I kept my journal, a journal of tears.

Heartbreak Town must have affected quiet, disciplined Dan in ways we did not understand. One of his college letters revealed a bitterness I never knew existed in this "too obedient" son.

"Christians aren't real," he wrote. "Just Christmas trees with ornaments, cut off from the stump, dying because of lack of connection between themselves and the stump. Don't write your letters about living 'close to the Lord.' Get off the throne and get down to help people, like Jesus did."

I cringed! Wasn't that what we had been doing in Heartbreak Town? Had he forgotten? And now does he lump us all together like Christmas trees? Oh, God, what's happening to our children?

Harold—come home! The scream was never heard.

Letters came from Jan, the one bright spot in this darkness. "Don't forget to pray for us—you are the most wonderful family in the world. I love you."

Harold wouldn't talk so I wrote notes and put them in his suitcase, pinned to his underwear, socks, and pajamas. In a lonely motel room he would read:

Harold darling,

Your verse has always been Jeremiah 33:3: "Call unto me—and I will show you mighty things."

You are dealing with God, Creator of Heaven and Earth. The same power that raised Jesus from the dead is given to you—for life.

The days are short and God wants you all the way. You are traveling in your own strength. Take time with God and get your direction from Him—saves time and money.

You are toiling all night and catching nothing. God will fill your net when you are obedient to His commands.

Let's call our family to prayer. We all need God's power these days.

We still have to choose whom we will serve. I'm not asking for material things—just for our family to be one.

> *I love you,*
> *Twinklex* [my nickname]

P.S. Please listen to God.

(Years later I found my letters tied together in his dresser.)

Darling Harold,

Life is like a dye that won't come out with washing. Events make a pattern and we can't always shuffle time and events like checkers.

You have so much to give—please don't wait for "someday."

The children have seen enough battles—now is time for victory.

I love you, and want only the best for you—not a shadow of what could be.

Love,
Twinklex

The grandchildren didn't know this Papa in the dark night of his soul. His children did come to understanding with the years, and they never gave up loving and praying.

I long for the young generation to know that in the storms of life we don't abandon ship—the Captain is at the helm.

God winds the clock.

28

The Wastebasket Journal

Today our pastor pronounced the benediction, and the congregation from Myrtle Grove Presbyterian Church in Wilmington, North Carolina, streamed into the parking lots, bound for home.

Our pastor emeritus Horace Hilton used to say, "Don't lose your Christianity in the parking lot. Be patient!"

I usually tried to slip out first, but it seemed I always managed to be one of the last. "If Chris and Mother wouldn't talk to a hundred people we could get home faster," Ralph would say.

Our new pastor, in his flowing robes, towered in the pulpit. His "thus saith the Lord" found an audience with open hearts to hear. His message today was from Habakkuk. "Oh Lord, I cried, and you didn't answer" (see 1:2). At the conclusion a hushed crowd listened to the benediction as the words echoed in my heart: "The silence of God doesn't mean God is not there."

I headed for the car, mentally checking my list: Put ice in the glasses, make gravy, mash the potatoes. Everyone had a task.

Into my heart crept the silent tread of memories from a long-ago time when both Harold and God seemed silent, when I cried in the night. Now Harold was Home—safe. God was silent, but I didn't cry. Why? I had learned to trust Him through the wilderness.

While the potatoes took a good beating, the gravy simmered, and the rolls were browning, Ralph came to me with some papers in his hand. "Mother, when dinner is over, I have something to show you."

"What?" My curiosity wouldn't wait.

"I found part of your journal in the wastebasket."

"What part?"

"Look, these papers were mixed in with some college papers I had discarded, but then I recognized your handwriting. Mother, I never knew how hard it was— I read some of this, and I just cried."

"Oh, no, these were supposed to be hidden, only for me to read. I can't believe they got mixed in with other papers."

"I think they should be published, Mother."

"Oh, no, I never intended to expose my heart in public."

"Mother, I can see hundreds of pastors, wives, single parents, and lonely people who think they are all alone in a wilderness. They need to know someone has been there and that God brought us through the valley; not only through the wilderness, but into a land of God's promises and joy. Put it in the book. Our children need to know that God is faithful, that even in the silence, He is there."

So it came to pass that I read again the journal from the wastebasket. This time I wept—not from grief, but from joy.

God had brought us through the wilderness and there is the sound of music coming from our home.

Harold had marked Psalm 89:15: "Blessed is the people that know the joyful sound: they shall walk, O LORD in the light of thy countenance."

I read someplace that sorrow makes places in the heart for joy. No wonder I could sing now—even though there was a time to cry.

From my journal:

Easter 1964

Tonight is Easter night. The lights from the friendly shopping center in Greensboro look like candles in the dark. The halls are quiet as nurses turn off lights and make bed-check rounds. The day has ended!

It began with a splash of light across the grey sky; then the morning sun filled the resurrection day with glory.

I had planned a pleasant morning—warm pecan rolls and coffee, and the table set for dinner. The turkey was ready by 7 A.M. The kitchen was spotless; curtains were hung at 2 A.M. Sleep came like the welcome of a warm blanket on a cold night.

I was engulfed in its luxury when the phone rang with clanging insistence. Emergency call, and I found myself heading into the morning sun with all the gloom of futility, caught in circumstances beyond my control.

I was angry! Tears of resentment blinded my eyes. I had asked for so little, just to be home and have breakfast with my family, and for us to attend Easter service together.

Other mothers would be dressed up in flowered hats and corsages, escorted by proud husbands, adoring sons and daughters. I walked alone into the presence of death—cold, clammy, icy death.

The sun mocked me through dusty windows while Easter music heralded the resurrection morning. I fought the enemy—death—and he gained, inch by inch.

Visitors filled the halls, and children with Easter baskets visited grandparents. Inside I felt cold and grey. Such a small wish—to sit in church with my own.

It's been a long day. Sixteen hours with death—cold, clammy, chilling death. This is resurrection day?

I am weary like the watchers at the tomb. The sun has long retreated behind darkened skies. The lights on the highway measure the darkness. Every nerve in me clamors for rest—long, sweet sleep. Yet the tomorrows are filled with more needs, more strain, more battles against fear and death.

Before I go to sleep I'll read the Easter story again. He who conquered death can conquer the tomorrows, with their fears and uncertainties.

This has been a long, lonely, disappointing day. Can this be God's will for me? Is this my Gethsemane, and how long will it last? Am I not to be loved and protected from the battle? Why is so much asked from me? Love, prayer, understanding, patience, the strength of a mule? Why?

Is the power of the resurrection not for us in our twentieth-century living? What hinders the answers to endless prayers to heaven? Do I work until I drop from exhaustion? Is there no other way?

Forgive me, Lord, for the luxury of self-pity. I'm so very human and so much a woman. I need to be loved and cherished and cared for. I need the warmth of the sun to make me blossom into fruition and creativity. But then, You made me. You know what I need.

Must I be watered by tears and the soil powdered by crushing defeats? Perhaps I couldn't stand too much sun and warmth—but please, Lord, just a little!

I love the moonlight and roses, music and candlelight, a little silk and softness. I'm tired of starched uniforms and white shoes. I long to be needed and loved for who I am, not what I can do.

I lean my weary head against the rough-hewn cross. My heart sees the darkness of men's wrongs. You didn't deserve it but You took my place. Take me out of self-pity and to the open tomb. Roll away my stone of doubt and let me look into the tomb and see the empty place. Sometimes in the darkness I search for You, and I cry, "They have taken away my Lord"—but just for the moment.

You promised never to leave me or forsake me. You are the Victor and the Peace, and You live in me. You are with me in darkness for You are the Light—so there can be no dark places.

My eyes are blind, but help me to see again the truths I know so well.

The cross is rough but I press my tear-stained cheek against its roughness. My eyes are dim but I see the empty tomb.

You sent the Comforter to dwell in us and all power is given to us. The long day is done, and the night wraps a blanket over the city.

Resurrection morning is in my heart.

Thank You, Lord Jesus, for being obedient to the cross, for triumphing over the grave, for giving us the Holy Spirit to indwell us with power. Help me to be obedient to walk in faith, in newness of life. Thank You, Father, Son, and Holy Spirit.

P.S. I'll be glad to come Home where the enemy can't enter. I want to see You, Jesus, to thank You, and I'm ashamed of self-pity. I just needed a little talk with You.
Please come soon!
The waiting is long and I am homesick for heaven.
Easter night, 1964
Wesley Long Hospital

(Another P.S. Twenty-seven years later I received a note thanking me for caring for someone's grandmother and "bringing hope and comfort to the family when God took her Home on Easter, in 1964.")

Another time when I needed the warmth of the sun to bring blossoms, it came through a camellia bush.

The bush had outgrown the space beside the front porch.

"Harold, please trim that bush—it's just too big."

The bush was an anniversary gift from Harold's parents, now Home with the Lord, and for years the bush of crimson flowers had beautified our yard.

One day, after hearing my urging once too often, Harold impatiently hacked away at the bush—then drove off to a meeting.

I stood in silence with unshed tears. My favorite bush was dead. Only brown twigs stuck out, ugly and bare. Now it needed to be dug up, but I waited for spring—and then another spring.

The winter came, and the snowflakes couldn't cover the brown twigs. The wind whipped against the ugly bush, but I couldn't take it out.

I felt like that bush—ugly, alone, and bare, with the wind whipping against my wounded spirit. For me, spring would never come.

A godly man, the patriarch of my day, gently urged me to confront Harold. But I was a peacemaker, a "fixer," and confronting was not part of my nature.

"Sometimes God asks us to do difficult things, to stand against a continuous wrong. Harold needs his family, and he loves his family. And I suggest an emotional shock treatment. Threaten him with the loss of his family unless he seeks help."

I did.

"*You must make a choice.*" I was quiet, but firm. "Perhaps you have heard me so much you can't hear God. Please go to some place quiet and alone and listen to God's still voice. You must make a decision—for us to be one and serve God as a family."

I watched Harold drive away with his suitcase and Bible. I stood, still quiet and firm, with a confidence not my own, as the car faded into the distance.

I closed the bedroom door and collapsed. What had I done? I fell on the floor and soaked the carpet with tears until there were no more tears. Clutching Harold's coat I cried, "My God, my God, don't forsake him. Speak, Lord, speak."

There was no more strength in me. It was then that God spoke to me through His Word. "I have loved you with an everlasting love and I will carry you between My shoulders."

Love lifted me! I was the wounded sheep in the arms of the Good Shepherd. I fell asleep.

Nights and days blurred into a misty fog, but the Good Shepherd *continued to hold me between His shoulders.* One night when I couldn't sleep, I sang to myself, "He hideth my soul in the cleft of the rock . . . And covers me there with His hand." Someone gently wrapped a soft blanket around me—then it was morning. Was it an angel?

The days continued to march in a disciplined routine, while my heart kept crying to God. Even in the silence He was there.

Another spring came and with shovel in hand I determined to remove that ugly bush.

My eyes blinked in the sunlight—I saw white tips on the twigs! "My bush is alive!"

I gazed in wonder.

I heard a step behind me. "Yes, the bush is alive and will bloom again. And so will we!"

Harold was home!

29

Heart's Cry

Also from my journal.

> Forgive me, Lord,
> But I can't see
> Beyond the cloud
> That hides Your face
> From me.
>
> Yesterday, I soared
> With eagle's wings.
> Faith topped mountains
> Where the valley
> Sings.
>
> Forgive me, Lord;
> I plummeted to earth,
> Passed by the clefts,
> The hiding place—rest
> And girth.

Forgive me, Lord,
But I can't hear
Your voice calling
Through this pounding
Fear.

Yesterday, I was warm
With plans and dreams,
A song of praise,
Melody of sunbeams,
Mountain streams.

Forgive me, Lord;
I don't understand
How faith can mount,
But doubt can hide
Your Hand.

I only know,
Although I cannot see,
I will believe
Your everlasting love
Holds me.

M.J.

Cry, But Not Too Long

I cry into the darkness,
And the velvet touch of night
Enfolds soft arms around me
To shield me from the light.

I reach into the spaceless sky
To clasp a falling star,
And trace a pathway in the night
And follow moonbeams far.

The summer wind sighs through pines
To sing a sad, sweet song
To blend with the night bird
While waiting for the dawn.

Life is filled with midnight,
Broken dreams, and falling stars,
An endless reaching for moonbeams,
A gift of love without scars.

I reach into the nighttime
For darkness soft and warm,
And wait with sighing pines
For the breaking of the dawn.

The dawn comes stealing through
The shadows of the night,
I brace myself for standing
Naked in the morning light.

When sunbeams play across my face
My tears run to hide.
A waiting day expects the brave
Sorrow's shadows to step aside.

I turn to face the sunlit day
With sounds of life and song,
And move with love to guide my way
From dawn to evening calm.

Crying in the wind.
I heard her, crying in the wind;
The pines sighed with the storm.

Tears in the rain.
I saw them, tears in the rain,
Splashed on her cheek, in the rain.

Sighing through the trees.
I heard her, sighing through the trees,
A broken heart, mourning in the dark.

Bending with the storm.
I saw her, bending with the storm,
Still standing, face to the wind.

Calling out my name.
I heard her calling out my name;
I turned and walked away.

Reaching out for me.
I felt her reaching out for me;
I moved, just beyond her touch.

Praying long for me.
I heard her praying long for me;
I heard, but walked away.

Silence now for me.
I hear only silence now for me;
I went too far— just beyond her reach.

Now, I am sighing in the wind.
Oh, God, I'm crying in the rain.
I turned away—too far—too long.

The Winter Wind

The cold wind beat against my stinging
  eyes
As hot tears fell.
The dry crackling leaves of the woods
Were echoes of the past;
Even the trees reached out empty arms;
The shelter of the leaves was gone.
The grey sky hung like a
Limp blanket overhead.

The silent cries from within my heart
Burst within me;
I kept running.
My legs ached;
The wind was cold;
I longed to reach for strong arms
To hold me close,
And ease the screaming hurt within.

I called for Mother, wishing to be a child,
To bury my head in her lap
And sob my heart out.
I'm alone.

The birds have their nests;
I wanted a shelter for my wounded spirit.
All the hurt piled into
One screaming grief.

There's a grief that grinds;
There is a sorrow that cuts clean
And can heal with time;
But there is a grief that twists and turns
Around and around,
And leaves no place for healing.
My prayers are choking sobs
That wail with the wind.
Too tired to move,
I leaned against the rough oak tree
And held it close.

"Sorrows were making places in the heart for joy."

The Secret

I didn't know
You waited patiently for me.
I didn't know
God loved me so.

I didn't hear
You calling in the noisy din.
I couldn't hear
For fretting fear.

I didn't see
Your outstretched hand across
  the way.
I couldn't see
Your plan for me.

Your spirit came
And whispered low,
Start praising child;
By faith you'll know.

"Faith hears the approaching footsteps of God's salvation."

—Charles Spurgeon

30

The Homecoming

"Grammy, you never finished the story. Did Papa ever go back to Heartbreak Town?" Katie was asking. "And that's not all. How did you get to Wilmington? Shawn, Eric and Sarah were born in Greensboro. Why wasn't I born in Greensboro?"

"I guess you will write a book someday since you know how to keep asking questions.

"One day your Papa talked to your Daddy and Mother about moving to Wilmington to start your Dad's own business. Sarah was a tiny baby when we all moved to Wilmington in 1978. You were born later, a very special Wilmington girl."

Kate remembered. "We lived in a blue house and I could ride my tricycle to Grammy's house. I told my friends how Daddy used to be a hippie but he gave his heart to Jesus."

Ralph grew wistful. "I've often wondered what happened to Dad after Heartbreak Town. Sometimes I think it was like an emotional stroke that paralyzed him from communicating his feelings.

"I'll never forget how he waited for me to come home when I was having such a bad time. He sat on the porch for three days and nights. Everyone else thought I wouldn't come, but he said, 'He'll come!' And I did.

"I promised I would never give up on Dad; he never gave up on me. What really happened to make Dad come home?"

Harold went to a motel and stayed for a month, alone and quiet. He really spent time in the Word and called for God's help. He was terrified of losing his family.

He fell asleep and had a dream. His entire life played before him like a video, and all through the years he saw God's love protecting him from danger. Then it was like he came out of a dark tunnel of failure, defeat and bitterness into the light of God's love and the love of his family.

"I was home again," he said.

Just as God poured out His love to Harold, even in the difficult times when he thought God was silent, so Harold poured out his love and joy to everyone he met. That is the man his grandchildren knew—a Papa who was always there for them, full of stories, a good listener and an encourager to all he met. He was never too busy for his children or grandchildren after that experience.

Harold encouraged me to write, and he told the publisher, "Margaret was my supporter for forty years; now it is my turn to do everything in my power to help her."

He did! He typed, edited, handled travel and schedules, and relieved me from details so I could write.

"But did Papa ever go back to Heartbreak Town?"

One day we received an invitation to a reunion—or homecoming—in Heartbreak Town.

"Daddy, you have to go—you just have to go." Jan rolled her pleading brown eyes and he melted before her gaze. "We'll drive together and you'll see how great it will be. We have to go back. Love and forgiveness are acts of the will, and we can be free."

We drove through the hills and valleys together and stopped at a beautiful home nestled in a forest. It looked like a picture from *Better Homes and Gardens*. Inside the house, beautiful antiques, paintings and polished floors revealed the creative, artistic taste of one of my "little choir girls" from thirty years ago.

The table was spread with colorful dishes, fancy casseroles and salads. The "youth choir" was there and sang the songs of long ago. One was "Every Day with Jesus Is Sweeter Than the Day Before."

Now they were parents and grandparents. One was a doctor and two were serving as missionaries. They were all making God visible, through their creative vocations, in the marketplace.

We laughed and cried and sang the old songs, and Harold was surrounded by his "church."

"See, Preacher, we didn't go anyplace. Look at us, still standing on the Solid Rock. We love the Lord, Preacher, and didn't forget what you taught us."

One mother whispered, "My daughter is an accomplished musician because of Janice."

"You said we could do anything! We did!"

Janice remembered when one of our best friends came to see us and asked Dad to read.

"No one reads Scripture like you do, Preacher."

Reverence filled the room as Harold read the Scripture. We all agreed no one could read the Word out loud like Daddy.

Unconditional love and forgiveness, the precious gold, tried by fire, weathered the storms and sailed over to the other side.

"What happened to the bad guys, Grammy?"

"Actually the 'bad guys' were few in number, but they did make a lot of noise. Most of them are dead now.

"Now the shell that Harold had retreated into crumbled, and bitterness and unforgiveness slithered away in defeat. Love had washed his heart clean!

"God had restored the years the locusts had eaten, and now Harold—and all of us—were really home.

"'Amazing grace! how sweet the sound,' echoed across the woods and over the lights of the city.

"There is a fountain where healing waters flow. It is called Calvary.

"Yes, Katie, we went back to Heartbreak Town, and someday I want to take you and your daddy, in fact all of you, back to the fork in the road.

"You, too, will hear the music."

31

The Promised Land

"Why are you giving Aunt Jan your cedar chest?"

"Well, Sarah, since Uncle Jud became president of Gordon College, Jan had to move into the president's home, called the Wilson House. It's a large rambling place with spacious rooms and long halls.

"The colorful Oriental rugs, priceless antiques, and paintings are part of the house, but Jan has to fill in some places with her own creative touch. The cedar chest will have the perfect place.

"At first Aunt Jan said, 'I'm a caretaker of an institution and I don't have a home; besides, I miss my Daddy. He'd come and help me.'"

"I guess we all miss Papa. He could always fix things." Sarah missed him, too.

"Jan left a lovely Cape Cod house to move into that large Wilson House, and she thought it would never feel like home. But you wouldn't believe how she made it 'home.' With your creative ability, you would appreciate how she gave an industrial kitchen a beautiful

Scandinavian look with gleaming white enamel cabinets, blue wallpaper, and touches of yellow. I can't wait to take you with me to see it.

"Not only did she make it 'home' for her family, but she also made it a place of welcome for the larger college family. With her humor, graciousness and warmth, she could host the Frisbee team one night, feeding them Kentucky Fried Chicken, and then hold a formal dinner the next night, or a picnic for four hundred."

"I'd like that." Sarah was impressed.

"That's not all, Sarah. The presence of the Lord was in that house, and I know God will bless them both."

So it came to pass that Ralph took the carved walnut cedar-lined chest to the shop to be restored. Jan would fill the chest with memories from Wilson House.

I cried when I saw the empty space.

"I felt like part of me went in that cedar chest, Sarah, because Papa gave it to me when I was nineteen years old. It has been my most treasured piece of furniture all these years. You used to dress up with the things you discovered in the 'treasure' chest as we called it. Now you and Katie will have to help me find new places for my treasures.

"When you get married, I'll give you the poster bed with the hand-carved ball and claw feet—the first one your Daddy made."

"Look at this, Grammy, Daddy's tiny sweater and baby cap—and look at these shoes! And here are the baby books and Aunt Jan's baby clothes."

"That's not all, Grammy. I saw Papa's love letters."

"You would, Katie!" This from Sarah. "Don't let her get them; she'll read them in school."

"Don't worry, Sarah, I will find a secret place for those letters. Katie won't get them." But the look on Katie's face asked me, "Someday, maybe?"

"We'll pack the wedding dress and veil in tissue paper—and look at my shoes! Size 5½, and now I wear 8½! Horrors!"

Katie ran off to dress up in my nurse's uniform from my student days—blue and white stripes, an apron, and black cotton stockings.

Sarah seemed to sense that not only "things" came out of the chest.

"It's not hard to find a place for things, Sarah, but memories won't go in a box; they keep coming out of hiding at the most unexpected times, and they make us laugh and cry."

"Oh, look, Grammy, here is Uncle Dan's tiny sailor suit. And Aunt Jan's organdy dress. Look at all the hand embroidery on it."

Sarah took off with a book of pictures, and I was left with a memory that wouldn't stay in the box.

It was a recent time, the summer of 1991. Harold and I walked on the pier of Wrightsville Beach, watched the fishermen pull in their lines, and scanned the distant horizon where sailboats were outlined against the sky.

We sat on a bench, and propped our feet on the rail, and watched the rolling waves. The surfers waited for the right wave, then rode in with the wind.

There is a tide in the affairs of men,
Which taken at the flood, leads on to fortune;

Omitted, all the voyage of their life
Is bound in shallows and in miseries."[1]

With my head on Harold's shoulder we sat quietly with our memories.

For me, it was as though the curtains parted on the horizon and the drama of our life rolled across the stage. We were so young, so ready to change the world in thirty days or less; then the little ones came in their Denton sleepers to crowd into our warm bed on a cold winter morning.

I could see Jan, the child of joy who was always planning surprises for the family, come on stage in a uniform, blowing a trumpet in the marching band; then in a ruffled dress for a piano recital; then in a wedding dress.

She always looked at the world with an "Alice in Wonderland" expression.

I saw Dan, praying for his brother in a far country— and Ralph came home!

Years later, Ralph came down the aisle, serving communion—an elder in his church! My heart still sings "Amazing Grace."

Somehow the wilderness years wouldn't focus. They faded into a mist, and only God's love and grace stayed on stage.

Harold broke the silence. "Margaret, we have come out of the wilderness wanderings into the promised land—Wilmington! How I love this place!

"We've worked together on eight books. Perhaps the world has heard more about God's faithfulness than I ever could have told from a pulpit.

"God alone can take the tides we missed and turn the shallows and the miseries into triumph."

The curtain closed; the sun set in all its splendor, and hand in hand we walked off the pier, toward our Wilmington home.

In October of 1991, Harold went to his heavenly Home—to the Father of all grace and mercy.

In the grey dawn I cried, "Who will wind the clock?"

It is now 1993, and I'm closing the pages of this book. The grandfather clock chimes midnight, which means dawn is not far away.

My times are in God's hands, and He winds the clock.

Epilogue

Let's Go!

It was September 1998 when Hurricane Bonnie unleashed wind and waves against our beautiful North Carolina shore.

From my office window I watched palm trees bend in the wind, then bravely rise again to face the sky.

The wind screamed like a freight train, tearing through the woods, then sobbed mournfully and slipped away with a sigh. Trees stood bare, leaves stripped from their branches—but we had survived another hurricane.

Storms do that to us too sometimes. They rip through our ordered lives until we are left to cry in the wind, stripped of courage to go on.

In 1991, when my cold wind blew, I felt bent like the palm tree, but God's grace, love and mercy became the wind under my wings, and I stood—and having done all—still stand. Because He lives, I can face my tomorrows.

After the long agonizing night in the Garden of Gethsemane, Jesus said to His disciples these simple words, "Let us go."

Somehow those words burned into me, and when I thought I couldn't face Christmas without Harold, I heard, "Let US go! You are not alone. Lo, I am with you always—even now."

I got up, put on an apron and baked the traditional Christmas bread.

My 16-year-old grandson Eric said, "Come on, Grammy—let's go—out-of-town basketball." So I ate pizza and hot dogs and went to the games.

When it was time for travel, Jan said, "Come on, Mother. Let's go."

Our pastor, Horace Hilton, was taking a group to the Holy Land, and once again I heard, "Let's go!"

What an experience to walk where Jesus walked and sense our own hearts burning within us on the Emmaus Road.

It took a year before I could work in my office; I felt like the palm tree bent to the ground—and so alone.

Ralph brought a beautiful black Doberman and she put her head in my lap and looked at me with those soulful eyes that said, "Let's go."

I finally went to the office, and I wrote *Who Will Wind the Clock?* in 1993.

Chris, my daughter-in-love, and I were on our way to Greensboro where I was to speak at a Christmas breakfast. We had gone a hundred miles (half the way) when a freak hurricane-type blizzard flung snow across our path. Cars stopped, and, terrified (we were Southerners, you know), we turned around and went all the way back home.

I finally found the presence of mind to call Greensboro and ask what the situation was.

We had stopped too soon. If we had gone just one or two miles further, we would have driven through the storm and seen sunshine on the other side.

We finally went back and did drive through the storm. After that, I wrote the book, *The Sun Is Shining on the Other Side* in 1994.

When Jesus and His disciples were in the storm on the Sea of Galilee, He said, "We are going over to the other side." He didn't tell them a storm would greet them on the way.

We don't get warnings—the storms seem to just burst upon us. It's then that we realize we are not made in a crisis, but we are revealed in a crisis. It is then we need to know that our hope is built on the Solid Rock, Christ Jesus.

In 1996 I wrote *All God's Children Got Robes*. One day I was dressed in velvet and lace; then a storm blew in and I found myself in a hospital see-through gown heading for cancer surgery.

Today I wear a garment of praise and thanksgiving for renewed health and strength.

In 1997 I wrote *A View from the Top*. A man of God had suffered a stroke and sat helpless in a wheelchair. He called his family together and sang the Doxology; then he added, "It has been a long, hard climb up this mountain, but I'm here to say, 'The view from the top is great!'"

That is faith!

This year, 1998, I was part of a Gordon College Tour to Greece and Turkey, where we followed the steps of Paul. Then a four-day cruise that ended at the Isle of Patmos.

Storms have a way of blowing into our lives through disaster, suffering and death, but at the end of the journey there will be a shout of victory—and sunshine!

My sister, Grace, became terminally ill in February, 1997, and we sang the hymns of faith until she went Home to be present with the Lord.

In December of the same year, Jeanelle, our youngest sister, went into God's presence while we all sang, "And we shall dwell in the house of the Lord forever."

Doris, my faithful prayer partner through all the years, now has Alzheimer's disease. In the midst of confusion, Joyce Solveig and I say, "Doris, we are going to sing." We pray for the children, and then we sing, "Surely goodness and mercy shall follow me all the days of my life."

Doris's spirit blends with our spirits and she says, "Yes, all together."

Out of six sisters (our precious baby sister Bernice had died of scarlet fever at the age of 2) and one brother, Joyce and I are left, and our heart's cry is to be faithful—not necessarily for books, or travel, or Bible teaching, but to show God's strength, His power and His love to this generation, to our children and our grandchildren.

That is why I pack my suitcase, get up at 4:30 A.M. to get the early flight, and go on traveling and speaking, because I love to tell the story of Jesus and His love.

One of these days we'll hear the trumpet sound and God will call His children Home . . .

Let's Go!

Notes

Chapter 1
1. Margaret Jensen, "You Can't Go Home Again," *First Comes the Wind* (San Bernardino, CA Here's Life Publishers, 1986), 161.

Chapter 4
1. Fanny J. Crosby, "All the Way My Saviour Leads Me."

Chapter 6
1. Edward Mote, "The Solid Rock."

Chapter 11
1. Robert Frost, "Stopping by Woods on a Snowy Evening."

Chapter 20
1. Shakespeare, *Julius Caesar*, Act IV, iii.

Chapter 23
1. Oswald Chambers, *My Utmost for His Highest* (Rahway, NJ: Dodd, Mead & Co., 1935), 361.

Chapter 24
1. Oswald Chambers, *My Utmost for His Highest* (Rahway, NJ: Dodd, Mead & Co., 1935), 366.

Chapter 31
1. Shakespeare, *Julius Caesar*, Act IV, iii.

Other Books by Margaret Jensen

ALL GOD'S CHILDREN GOT ROBES
Hundreds of thousands of readers enjoy Margaret Jensen's wit and wisdom shared from her heart as she relates poignant and humorous stories to powerfully illustrates God's faithfulness and provision.

FIRST WE HAVE COFFEE
First We Have Coffee is Margaret Jensen's poignant and humorous collection of real-life stories about growing up in an immigrant Norwegian Baptist pastor's home. In this, her first book, Margaret tells her beloved stories of Mama, her Norwegian immigrant mother, whose open heart and home touched many. This heartwarming book is filled with godly wisdom, humor, heartaches and nostalgia.

LENA
Lena is a true story of family reconciliation, showing the remarkable contribution of a college campus maid whose prayers, stories, and songs uplifted students and staff alike. One of Margaret Jensen's most popular books, it tells the inspiring account of how one woman's faith helped heal Margaret's troubled family.

A NAIL IN A SURE PLACE
Master storyteller Margaret Jensen delivers powerful examples of the dramatic ways God uses people to answer prayer. "We are all nails," explains Jensen, "all here for someone to hang on to." She shares the secrets to joy and strength in all situations.

PAPA'S PLACE
Delving into her childhood, Margaret Jensen shares God's compassion and grace in this message of hope and renewal through a loving, merciful Lord. With wit and inviting warmth, Margaret shares about her papa—used mightily by God despite his fierce temper and other shortcomings.

A VIEW FROM THE TOP
With wisdom garnered from a lifetime, beloved storyteller Margaret Jensen looks back on her life and what she has learned about prayer, grace, faithfulness, and walking in the power of God. These humorous, poignant stories warm the heart and inspire the soul to seek God's comfort.